FORCE

A NO-HOLDS-BARRED INSIDER'S VIEW OF BOXING

Robert McAdam

© 2017 Robert McAdam

Sugarrays Publications
Vancouver, British Columbia, Canada

All rights reserved, including the right of reproduction of text and images in whole or in part in any form.

REVISED JULY 2017

Cover image: Jack Dempsey

Dedicated to Catherine;
my soul mate, inspiration and true love.

Table of Contents

Foreword 1

Introduction 2

Background 4

How We Got Here: The Early Dsays 13

Training & Technique Past & Present 70

Fighters and Features in Force: An Album 158

Acknowledgements 187

Foreword

Robert McAdam gives a frank examination of the underside of the sport and reveals its inherent dangers.

He shatters the sanctity of Olympic and Amateur boxing, exposing what he considers to be their catastrophic effects.

He reveals the blunt realities of cheating, corruption and manipulation of both fighters and the public.

The latter part of the book offers one of the most comprehensive and insightful explanations of boxing training available in print.

McAdam was a boxer, a professional trainer, a qualified physical training instructor, a weight training instructor, a boxing judge (both amateur and professional), a referee, a cut man, a corner man, a manager of fighters, and the owner of cutting-edge boxing gyms. He has trained recreational, amateur and professional fighters, countless athletes, and even superstars.

Whether you're a fighter, a fan, or simply curious, his account will draw you in. There's no use fighting it!

Introduction

Amateur and Olympic boxing have crippled the sport.

Incorrect scoring and biased judging have acted as catalysts for profoundly flawed training that is tailored to satisfy points rather than the traditional standard of effective aggression.

The sport has been further damaged at the Olympic level by accusations that financial donations have compromised judging. As a result, there has been a steady decline in interest in both participation and viewing.

Professional boxing is on a roller coaster: huge public interest, jaw dropping decisions, inactivity in championship terms; and yet, the largest televised fight event of all time, on May 2, 2015, between Pacquiao and Mayweather, generated $410 million in the U.S. alone on pay-per-view.

Mixed Martial Arts (MMA) has worked tirelessly and very effectively to establish their sport, creating the illusion that their fighters are household names. Announcers froth at the mouth with frenzied superlatives about every next show. I believe they even use script writers to ensure each fight has optimized the angles of interest for both fight and fighters; the commentary is really very good.

Professional boxing has had to respond with fly-on-the-wall shows that allow a dimension hitherto unseen in the buildup to fights; so perhaps the competition is a good thing.

Boxing is an excellent form of defence. Having stood the test of time, it has a wonderful pedigree. It is embedded in our DNA, and perhaps that is the reason it has survived.

It has been said by one writer that there was a time when you could become the Heavyweight Champion of Canada if you owned a pair of gloves and got a letter from your mother.

Those days are long gone and the opportunity to succeed may be through a very small window, and that's only if you have the ability, skills, training, management, finances, and tenacity to make it.

There is no mention of luck here. In my experience, you cannot rely on luck. There is more bad luck than good luck in boxing, so, if you are relying on luck, take up poker.

We will visit trust, loyalty and politics, as they are tested.

In the following chapters, I will address virtually all aspects of boxing and ponder many issues, including the aforementioned amateur and professional judging and training, which require serious attention.

This book touches on unusual, contentious and interesting areas normally discussed only inside the rarified atmosphere of the gym among grizzled trainers like myself.

Robert McAdam

Background

A rabbi and a priest are sitting pre-fight ringside.
Both fighters are in the ring.
One of the fighters takes a knee
and makes the sign of the cross.
The rabbi asks, "What does that mean?"
The priest replies, "Fuck all if he can't box."

F = ma, Newton's second law of motion.

Force results from mass being multiplied by acceleration, and in boxing that must be through the target. Boxing is governed by the laws of physics. We cannot depend upon divine intervention.

Many years ago I met an elderly Grand Master of Oriental martial arts. He had been thrown out of his organization for failing to confirm that he had witnessed other Grand Masters demonstrate the "one-inch punch." The laws of physics apply to all martial arts.

Subsequently Newton's equation has played a direct part in the demise of martial arts gyms worldwide that operated under the conviction that speed alone will do the job.

A little about me:

I was born and raised in the North of England. As a youngster, I sucked at ball sports, but I loved boxing even as a child, and started training on my own long before I could go to a boxing gym.

I trained in play areas and parks at night and ran miles every day, often wearing a bin liner (garbage bag) because I could not afford a sweat suit. Later, I continued to use them because they are easily discarded after use with no need to launder. It got to the stage that if I did not train, I could not sleep.

I did hundreds of sit-ups and push-ups every week for years without fail. I could do 90 full push-ups in 60 seconds and, to get extra depth, I used house bricks. A brick doubled as a weight behind my head for sit-ups. Some days, I would do a thousand sit-ups at a time. I could do 80 tricep dips. Sometimes I would even run with house bricks; I was on a very limited budget, and old bricks were free.

I did not know anything about the local football teams, but could tell you all about boxing and the history of fighters past and present. I was captivated by boxing and watched it on TV at every opportunity.

As soon as I could, I went to the best boxing gym in my city - Newcastle. The gym was typically located in one of the less salubrious areas. It involved two buses across the city to get to the gym, and youngsters often threw rocks at the bus for entertainment as it ran the gauntlet. When I didn't have the bus fare, I would run. It took over two hours to get there.

At that time, the City of Newcastle provided industrial strength adjustable boards for the windows of domestic properties because they also benefitted from a good stoning between buses. The owners got used to living in the houses in their boarded state, so the houses remained that way.

Grainger Park was a combined youth club and boxing gym that provided a haven for youngsters with nowhere to go in a rough area enjoying hard times.

One of the first boys I met in the gym was Billy, a black-haired, stocky kid. He had a 90-degree indent in the skin where the cartilage should have merged with the bone of his nose. When I asked him about it, he said, "Mi Fatha hit me with a cricked bat." His dad had used the edge, which must have been life threatening. I did not ask why. It was Grainger Park, and no further explanation was offered.

The gym accommodated some of the toughest boys, men and trainers in the city. Most had been comfortable with, and accomplished at, street fighting long before they took up boxing.

My trainer, Norman, was a tough older guy who owned a fruit and vegetable business. He was overweight, and he wore a toupee that no one ever mentioned under any circumstances. He looked like a bulldog chewing a wasp and never smiled unless he absolutely had to. There was a smouldering certainty that things would turn very bad very quickly if that wig was mentioned by anyone. He oozed menace.

Norman loved to get the beginners into the boxing ring to move around with him, but mostly to see how they responded to a good punch on the nose.

I took a friend along once who became the unlucky recipient of Norman's crushing left. He got out of the ring bleeding and could barely focus due to his eyes watering. It was a perfect shot right between the eyes. Forty-five years later, my friend still remembers it like yesterday. He did not return, and I am sure Norman was convinced that he had done a great job, weeding out some chaff.

The boxing ring was set to one side of a hall, which accommodated the gym. This meant it was actually close to a wall on two sides, and you had to be careful not to get knocked through the ropes or you would hit your head on the wall. This, I was to find over the years, was a common feature of boxing gyms. The ring was home-made, about 14' square and just off the floor. After the warm-up, coaching and bag work, it was on to the sparring, which was always very tough.

One dark night at about 10:30 p.m., whilst I was leaving the gym, a collection of six or seven thugs had congregated outside. They were entertaining themselves by bullying a youngster, and, as I left, I said,

"Leave him alone."

The thugs turned on me, and I backed back into the reception area of Grainger Park with one of the guys taunting, "Wanna fight? Wanna fight?" whilst poking me in the chest.

Almost imperceptibly. I nodded at the bullied youngster, and he locked the door behind the last of them as they followed me in. The next time the thug asked, "You wanna fight?" I said "Absolutely!" Just as he said "What?" I hit him hard.

There were only a couple of fighters left inside, and we destroyed the gang. Norman watched, and I think we must have looked like terriers having a great time with rats.

Being a member of Grainger Park stood for something. Messing with the fighters was a serious mistake.

The fight in the reception was an unexpected bonus that night. No big deal. There were other clubs in Newcastle, some closer. However, Grainger Park was my gym, and I was proud to be a fighter at that club. Being a member at that time automatically meant you were above average.

After leaving school, I moved to Warwickshire and joined Stratford ABC. It was located, coincidentally and conveniently, in the next street to my home, I trained and fought for that club but had to find work further afield.

I focused on getting a job in a commercial gym and sent my resume to 30 gyms in Warwickshire. I received three polite letters of refusal and one interview at Arena Fitness Academy, Coventry. Unfortunately, I did not get the job, and I was gutted.

Shortly after the interview, and purely by coincidence, the gym owner, Wadge, and Steve Early (an excellent local professional fighter) attended a show in which I was boxing in Coventry. Wadge came to the changing area to say hello, and I was both pleased and surprised to see him as I got ready to fight. When he asked what I thought about my fight, I told him the guy was much bigger, but to bet on me. My friends had won money betting on the results of my fights; just small bets made at the tables between spectators.

Because of the size difference when I went to the centre of the ring, the referee asked my weight. Before the fight, I was exactly 147 pounds, and the referee told me it was a middleweight fight, 165 pounds and up.

In the second round, the opposing corner threw in the towel, indicating they wanted to retire their fighter because he was taking a bit of a hiding. When I say "threw in the towel," usually the trainer climbs up to the ringside and waves the towel. It might not be seen if it is simply tossed into the ring.

Wadge rushed to the changing room and offered me a full time job at Arena Fitness Academy as an instructor, following training. What a great night! My debt to boxing was accumulating. It had just changed my life.

I moved to Coventry and immediately joined Tile Hill Boxing Club, to train with Billy Duffin, who was possibly the best trainer in the U.K.

I had beaten a very tough fighter from Tile Hill Boxing Club. I believe that he was NABC Champion, and he took three standing counts, one in each round, but did not go down. That was the first time I had hit a fighter really hard and he had stayed vertical. I thought I was losing my punching power. In all the time I was at Tile Hill, he and I never spoke more than a couple of sentences to each other, primarily because we may have had to fight again, but that did not happen.

On my first training session at Tile Hill, at the end of the night, a fighter named Murphy had a piece of wood between his teeth connected to a rope attached to another piece of wood threaded through 45-pound Olympic plates. He was nodding, lifting the plates over and over with his neck. I smiled and walked out. Murphy's neck was as strong as most people's legs.

Tile Hill was a council estate with a mixture of low income property and squalid high rise apartments. I secured accommodation in a high-rise very near the gym in Tile Hill. It was nasty, and the lift always smelt of urine, but I was as happy as I could possibly be; it was just a three-minute walk to the gym.

Billy told me some council house (regional property) inhabitants actually burnt the floorboards in rooms to keep warm in the winter. They fed the boards onto the fire and subsequently had to gingerly navigate their way around the rooms because of the missing flooring.

The boxing gym was located at the back of Tile Hill Social Club, which was a mecca for locals who spent most of their wages on beer at this recreational gold mine. The rest was spent at the local fish and chip shop, strategically located nearby and built like a bunker. The lives of a lot of locals involved alternating between those two buildings most every day, and that was how they spent all their money. These social clubs had melamine tables that were durable and quick to wipe, and the quantity of beer consumed was simply staggering.

My uncle told me with pride that he could remain at the bar at his social club, only leaving at closing time, but he had to get up every hour on the hour to go to the toilet. A rather curious pride, dedication to drinking and loyalty to the clubs existed within social club members.

In the U.K., amateur boxing shows always ended with food provided by the club that put on the show. This meant that everyone ate a meal together. It could be a simple sandwich and chips, or sometimes even a cooked complete dinner. It very much depended on the venue and wealth of the club, but it was traditional. Most fighters had to make weight on the night of the fight, and consequently we did not have too much to eat before competing. The meal was an opportunity for everybody to mix. It's unfortunate that this does not occur in Canada.

At one show I fought a guy who, whilst extremely brave, lost every round. In those days, I was 147 pounds, the rounds were three minutes, and we wore eight-ounce gloves and no head guards. As the fight progressed, the doctor was called to the ring several times to check on my opponent. I made the decision to let him survive the final round as he had been very brave. After the fight, in the middle of the ring, the referee raised his hand and there was uproar at his home show. When it was time to pick up our trophies the winner went first. I too, received a winner's trophy.

Later, I sat and ate a meal with the man, and he said he did not feel he won the fight. I did not tell him about the trophy, and to this day he still does not know. That might have been one of very few occasions in the U.K. in a real fight when both fighters received winner's trophies even though the fight was not close to being a draw.

I have learned a great lesson. Don't rely on the judges to get it right; take them out of the equation if possible.

When I was a young amateur, I sometimes received envelopes containing my "expenses," even though I travelled in the same vehicle as everybody else. At the time, any kind of funding was frowned upon because amateur meant amateur. However, clubs did this because I was low on funds. Some clubs wanted me to fight, and the money was quietly handed to me. I was grateful to every club for that kindness and have never forgotten it.

I have had a tremendous amount of fun, met some really wonderful people and made a modest living through boxing. I have tried to give back to the sport. Although I did not become a celebrated champion, I fought all over the U.K. and overseas. I never got knocked out or knocked down, and I feel privileged to have been involved in virtually all aspects of this sport.

I fought the Royal Navy champion, representing the Standard Triumph Select Team in Coventry. Although I was the local fighter, the Navy fighter came in second accompanied by a bagpiper. It was deafening and impressive, and any edge helps. Twenty-eight days earlier I'd had a suspension for a hideous cut caused by a deliberate head-butt while boxing for the County against Liverpool. The fighter spun around and head-butted with the back of his head. As I stood in the ring, I had to decide if I was going to protect my eye or go for it. As the bell rang I thought "Fuck it. Fortune favours the brave." I beat the Navy fighter with constant pressure, offering no opportunity to reopen the cut.

I found out something about myself that night, as it took a lot of resolve to go forward injured. You are unlikely to win if your primary focus is on survival.

It would be fair to say that I am the product of the tough gyms I attended. Some even had rat traps along the edges of the walls, but I loved those gyms, I truly respected the trainers and training that I received at every club. I am able to write this book as a result of my experiences over the years and because of the help of people who invested time and effort purely for the love of the sport.

Over fifty years of experience qualifies me to write this book - plus the fact that I own a gym. It's not just any gym. At times, it has been the largest boxing gym (by membership) in the world. I own Sugarrays Professional Boxing Gym. For years, we operated 24 hours a day, and thousands of people from all walks of life passed through its doors. We offer cutting edge training with old school grit, attention to detail, and genuine value for money.

Boxing is about fractions of a second. It's about subtle angles. It's about minute details combined with brutal force, skill, will, strategy, the ability to adapt. All the time the other guy is trying to beat you, but you have got to win.

This is no game. It's serious. You may get hurt, and many do - some permanently - and we will address that. The sweet science can be extremely bitter.

Boxers do not tap out. The option simply does not exist as it does in mixed martial arts. By convention, many fighters elect to go out on their shield, something that is brutal to witness and a magnificent demonstration of integrity wrapped in bravery.

Boxing gyms are special places, hallowed places, consecrated by the tremendous effort of all who went before.

Generations of fighters, trainers, hopes, dreams and achievements, the very DNA of ambition lurk in the gym. You can feel it. You can smell it.

The atmosphere, the smell, the broken and worn out equipment, rivalled only by the condition of the trainers, make boxing gyms unique and special places. High tech no, but cutting edge, absolutely.

I have lived and slept in them, but I never thought for one second that I would be involved in boxing my entire life. It has been wonderful.

I am a throwback. I know that. I come from a time and place where experience was earned the hard way and not acquired online.

We do not copy. It makes me cringe to see trainers choreographing pad work as the Mayweathers do, totally failing to appreciate it's done for publicity. Once the cameras go, he works on that beautiful, world-class jab and real punches, and you don't see the hours done there.

How We Got Here: The Early Days

Fist fighting has been a way to resolve disputes for as long as we have been able to clench a fist.

Ancient Sumerians practiced pugilism earlier than 3000 B.C.. In 900 B.C., Greeks made pugilism popular and bound the contestants' hands with a leather thong called a "cestus" (See image at the end of this section). The thongs inflicted massive damage. Later, gladiators wore spikes on their hands, and, seated face-to-face, fought to the death. One gladiator was credited with having killed 1,425 challengers before he succumbed.

After eventually recognizing the brutality of the cestus, The Romans banned it and converted pugilism back to a standing position. Later, bare-knuckle fighting was also banned.

Bare-knuckle fighting was revived in England by James Figg in 1719, and it flourished once again. It was documented that Figg had 2000 members in his club, making it a huge gym. He taught fighting with staffs and cudgels, as well as pugilism (boxing).

Orthodox or Southpaw

When James Figg (1684-1734) developed his school, he had his fighters lead with their right hand. His successor, Jack Broughton (1704-1789), elected to hold the dominant hand in reserve for power and a better coordinated defence. This has remained the norm. However, some fighters elect to lead with the dominant hand for extra power. Conversely some trainers make orthodox fighters southpaw for the perceived advantage as there are fewer of them. Only one in 10 is left handed.

Southpaw is a boxing term that designates the stance where the boxer has his right hand and right foot forward, leading with right jabs, and following with a left cross right hook. Southpaw is the normal stance for a left-handed boxer. The corresponding designation for a right-handed boxer is orthodox, and is generally a mirror-image of the southpaw stance.

The technique for punching differed in unprotected bare-knuckle fighting to avoid serious damage to hands in protracted fights. Some fights continued to the finish, while others had a specified number of rounds. It was possible for fighters to win fights but to sustain injuries that prevented further contests due to permanent hand injuries that ended their careers.

From the late 1800s to the early 1900s, the focus of fighting moved to the United States. Facing little competing entertainment and offering the thrill of the spectacle, boxing was supported by the public. Although it was outlawed in every state, news of fights carried far and wide. Famous fighters of the day drew crowds to watch and perhaps wager at events that were held outdoors or in warehouses or halls.

Fighters raked blows across the brow ridges of their opponents' faces to produce cuts to blind opponents with their own blood. Some fighters deliberately dropped their heads to absorb blows with their foreheads in order to damage the hands of their adversaries. The technique is still used in professional boxing to this day, and it is very effective. Vicious elbows, being thrown to the ground, and thumbing eyes all played a part.

Years ago, during fights of incredible length, fighters sometimes elected to turn their heads slightly, preferring to ride a blow on an ear and avoid facial damage that could drastically reduce the chance of success in the later rounds. This is one reason why the old pugilists had heavily cauliflowered ears in etchings.

In Britain, pugilists who were unable to continue in the later rounds of fights protested that they were blind, but not beaten. Actually they were beaten if they could not continue, despite being game.

I trained a man who fought in Ireland in a cage fight. He received massive approval and huge applause from the crowd as he had "Gameness" tattooed right across his chest, written in a large elaborate scroll. Unfortunately, the crowd thought it said "Guinness."

In 1882, American "Boston Strong Boy", John L. Sullivan, knocked out Paddy Ryan in the USA to win the world championship. Sullivan won 59 consecutive fights by knockout, fighting some of the most brutal contenders available. John L Sullivan was actually the first sports superstar.

"No contest" decisions could occur when fights got broken up or disrupted by authorities, or when draws or disqualifications caused unsatisfactory results. Sometimes the fighters reconvened at an alternative location to resolve matters a day or so later.

To this day, there are still bare-knuckle fights in some countries, and the fighters are sometimes kicked by the crowd to stand up if they go to the ground and begin to wrestle. I trained a man who fought under such circumstances in Siberia. Adin was an unusual guy. I fixed him up for a blind date with a hairdresser in Sweden, and before the meal I said, "Think of something interesting to talk about at dinner."

As we all sat to eat, he paused and announced, "This reminds me of the time I slaughtered a camel." I was panicking. It was totally unexpected, we were on the ropes, and I said, "That must have been awful." Trying to defuse the tension, he said, "Yes, I was looking into its eyes as I cut its throat." Well, that was the end of his date - KO round one in the first 10 seconds. He is probably single to this day.

In 1892, after 20 rounds, the title moved from John L Sullivan to the more scientific James J. Corbett under Marquess of Queensberry Rules. This was the first world championship with fighters wearing gloves, and a new era of boxing had begun.

A point of historical interest is that boxing created cinema. The first ever motion picture released was of an 1897 boxing match: Corbett vs. Fitzsimmons in Carson City, Nevada. Fitzsimmons won. In 2012, the film was added to the National Film Registry at the Library of Congress.

"I was a pretty good fighter. But it was the writers who made me great." -Jack Dempsey

Modern Boxing

Boxing can be formally defined as a combat sport requiring gloves to punch, conducted in a boxing ring, governed by a referee and officials under strict rules, judged on effective aggression, organized by weight and decided by decision or stoppage.

That description is accurate but does not begin to convey the impact of boxing.

Boxing has defined individuals, galvanized nations and created idols who have transcended time.

Controversies over the results of fights, arguments over who is best currently or in any given era, and the sometimes inflammatory remarks of trainers, fighters and fans make boxing truly compelling.

During major fights, scholars, leaders, white and blue collar workers, men, women, and children unite transfixed.

As modern boxing developed in the United States and evolved from bare-knuckle fighting, rules were gradually implemented and it became socially acceptable. Gloves, originally introduced to protect faces during sparring were incorporated in competition, specifically to protect hands and to enable fighters to extend their careers.

At the time, bare-knuckle fighters raised serious concerns that the force of punches would increase dramatically with the introduction of gloves, and time has confirmed that the bare-knuckle fighters were right. Sadly, the sport averages two deaths per year worldwide, despite ongoing efforts to ensure the safety of fighters.

The Marquess of Queensberry Rules

In 1865, John Graham Chambers drew up twelve rules to govern the conduct of boxing matches.

Chambers found a sponsor in John Sholto Douglas, who gained lasting fame simply by lending his name and initiating the end of the bare-knuckle fighting era. Douglas's title in the Peerage of Scotland was the Marquess of Queensberry.

Rule 1.
To be a fair stand-up boxing match in a 24-foot ring, or as near to that size as is practicable.
Rule 2.
No wrestling or hugging.
Rule 3.
The rounds must be of three minutes in duration, and one minute time between rounds.
Rule 4.
If either man falls, through weakness or otherwise, he must get up unassisted, 10 seconds to be allowed him to do so, the other man meanwhile to return to his corner, and when the fallen man is on his legs the round is to be resumed and continued until the three minutes have expired. If one man fails to come to the scratch in the 10 seconds allowed, it shall be in the power of the referee to give his award in favour of the other man.
Rule 5.

A man hanging from the ropes in a helpless state, with his toes off the ground, shall be considered down.
Rule 6.
No seconds or any other person to be allowed in the ring during the rounds.
Rule 7.
Should the contest be stopped by any unavoidable interference, the referee to name the time and place as soon as possible for finishing the contest; so that the match must be won and lost, unless the backers of both men agree to draw the stakes.
Rule 8.
The gloves to be fair-sized boxing gloves of the best quality and new.
Rule 9.
Should a glove burst, or come off, it must be replaced to the referee's satisfaction.
Rule 10.
A man on one knee is considered down, and if struck is entitled to the stakes.
Rule 11.
That no shoes or boots with springs be allowed.
Rule 12.
The contest in all other respects to be governed by the revised rules of the London Prize Ring.

The rules remained in force until 1920 when New York State legalized boxing and devised its own regulations.

"It is very much better for the young, as well as the old, to possess the knowledge of the manly art of self-defence than it is to have them resort to knives and guns." -John L. Sullivan

Boxing Gloves

The sole purpose of wearing gloves is to protect the athletes' hands.

To this day, some competition gloves are made with horse hair, and these carry a guarantee for a limited number of rounds if they are used in competition. Cleto Reyes of Mexico make such gloves, and these are generally preferred by punchers as it is believed that they cause more damage (cuts) to the opponent because of their construction.

It is widely thought, and my opinion, that the best make of gloves, head guards and mitts is the Japanese company, Winning. They produce superb equipment, with some of their laminated foams protected by patents. The superior quality, however, comes at a very high price.

Rival, a Canadian company owned by training legend Russ Amber, produces top quality and innovative equipment at a great price point. We carry Rival and use it in our boxing gyms.

Years ago, Jack Dempsey asked a swimwear company famed for the durability of its products to make him a head guard. Everlast did so, and it became a billion-dollar manufacturer of fight equipment. If you think about it, Everlast is an appalling name for a sporting goods manufacturer; however, quality and durability instantly overcame misgivings, and Everlast remains one of the most successful producers of boxing equipment on the planet.

Warning: the quality of gloves available does vary dramatically.

Ensure that the weight of the gloves, normally shown in ounces on a tag or printed on the glove, is accurate. It hardly ever is in my experience. I went into a retail martial arts store once, and not one pair of 16-ounce gloves weighed 16 ounces. A dozen or so brands were all too light. I have purchased around 12,000 pairs of gloves over the years and know that the weight of the gloves is too often incorrect; sometimes way out.

Gloves for competition: 6-ounce, 8-ounce, 10-ounce leather.
Tough man, white collar and some charity contests: normally 16-ounce or 18-ounce.
Training gloves: 16-ounce, 18-ounce, 20-ounce leather.

Specific bag gloves: 16-ounce, 18-ounce.

The lining for modern gloves is usually impact moulded foam. In the high-end gloves, it may be laminated. Horse hair would be quite unusual for training due to the very limited warranty.

For safety, gloves should always have the thumb attached to the main section. The gloves are secured at the wrist by Velcro or laces. In training Velcro is more prevalent for convenience; in competition, laces are more commonly used.

When I was a youngster at Grainger Park, Velcro had not yet been used on boxing gloves, so the only way to secure them was by laces. Nobody had their own gloves, so we used these huge old leather gloves, saturated with sweat through use, complete with sodden laces that we rammed inside the glove to save time, as they were communal. We had to hold the laces tight inside the gloves to secure them to spar, and this also facilitated a quick transfer to the next combatant. They were truly disgusting, but the idea of owning my own gloves never occurred to me due to the cost. The gloves had a distinct odour. Was it possible a rodent had crawled inside and curled up and died? When the gloves became sodden, that smell was transferred to anyone hit by them. You could taste it, and it clung to your skin long after the gloves came off.

In Sweden, I used to put the gloves outside in the sub-zero temperature to kill the bacteria causing the smell. Some folks use Febreze or Lysol; some buy glove dryer.

"He can run but he can't hide." -Joe Louis
(Regarding his forthcoming contest with Billy Conn)

Boxing Rings

The boxing ring in which matches now take place was originally a tramped-down circle formed on the ground by the shuffling feet of spectators at bare-knuckle matches. It later became a circle marked on the ground, and still later, a circle drawn inside a square roped area where boxers met to initiate each round.

It is now a commercially-built elevated square enclosed by four ropes. Competition rings are generally 16 to 24 square feet in area, measured from rope to rope, with an extra floor area outside the rope to provide footing and safety for fighters inside. When first entering a boxing ring, many people are surprised at how small the area is - claustrophobically small. A couple of steps and you are on the ropes.

The size of the ring can play a role in the success of a boxer, and fighters may stipulate the ring dimensions in the contract for a bout. Generally, pressure fighters prefer a smaller ring, while boxers with long reaches tend to favor larger rings. This is, of course, a generalization, and many factors may determine the ideal ring size for a particular fighter. Most boxers train in 16 to 20 foot rings at floor level, slightly above the floor, or a fully-elevated level, depending on the gym. Ideally 18 feet would be best.

Some early elevated rings were dangerously high, built to provide spectators with a good view of the action as they stood in the open watching. Access was by ladder. The height of the ring could contribute to a very serious fall should a fighter be knocked through the ropes (see image at the end of this section).

Sometimes temporary stands were erected, and, with the fear of collapse, fights had to start early, such was the demand. Tex Rickard (1870-1929), a famous U.S. promoter, had a large stand made of unseasoned (green) timber for one fight. The day was hot and sunny and many people had their suits ruined by sap from the wood.

Boxing rings today have canvas or vinyl floor covering. Canvas affords fighters better grip and leverage to hit. Canvas floor coverings are painted occasionally with an antibacterial paint and then look good as new. Advertisements are often placed on floor coverings, reducing traction in those areas. The dangerous result is that fighters sometimes slip.

Sugarrays' training rings now have rubber surfaces, which are non-slip even when wet and are fair to all combatants.

Vinyl (tarp) surfaces are used, but are treacherous because they are slippery when wet. Often a vinyl surface is used for training.

Heavier punchers are at a disadvantage when fighting in open air events, where moisture on the flooring can reduce traction. That applies to any flooring where traction is altered.

Interestingly, it is possible by looking at a group of fighters' boxing boots to determine which are the heaviest punchers based only on the wear on their boots (they have to be well worn). Soles are worn down by the pressure of fighters' feet as they drive home their blows, and the location of the wear indicates heavier hitters.

At one point in the 1940s, ship builders constructed a circular ring of aluminum tubing, covered in velvet. The round ring did not take off; however, it was a terrific effort (see image at the end of this section).

The added dynamic of corners really assists the spectacle - so long as it's not your fighter trapped in there. There are two corners - one with red and one with blue corner pads (by convention), with two diagonally opposite white padded corners referred to as the neutral corners. A fighter should be sent to the neutral corner by the referee whilst the referee is dealing with the opponent for whatever reason. I attended one show where the ring had one red and one green corner, but that was once in 50 years.

The four ropes (usually steel cables now) are tensioned by large turnbuckles anchored to the four sturdy corner posts. They are covered to protect the fighters, and are strapped top to bottom at regular intervals to help prevent fighters from falling out of the ring.

There is a floor area projecting outside the ropes, known as the apron, that offers a degree of safety and permits a fighter to remain in balance "on the ropes." It affords extra space for the rear foot, with the leg against the bottom rope. Corner men officials and others access the ring or stand outside the ropes on the apron.

Should a fighter fall through the ropes, the apron might offer a safety margin. This depends on the width of the apron; however, that seems to vary. Recently (2017), Bernard Hopkins took a nasty fall from the ring and was lucky not to be seriously injured. The apron looked quite narrow to me and he barely touched it as he fell to the ringside landing dangerously.

All competing fighters should test the tension of the ropes from inside the ring prior to fighting by leaning on them and should move around to test the bounce and traction underfoot, because it varies every time. I have had the ropes tightened during the interval of shows so that opponents cannot obtain advantage.

The ring superstructure may be constructed in many ways, and there are a variety of flooring materials and corner designs. Generally, the posts are over five feet in height, and if the floor is elevated, the posts would be eight feet or more.

A ring can have differing qualities each time it's assembled. There is no uniform measure for rope tension at present.

There are many kinds of cushion and foam underlays used to provide slight cushioning under the floor covering. For training, I like a 12-foot pound foam, thick to force and hard on the legs, forcing the fighters to work.

Rounds

Rounds (duration of competition) are predominantly two or three minutes in length, with a 60-second rest at the end of each round.

The number of rounds and their duration are dictated by event which is either professional or amateur and the level of competition.

Fights can take place over 12, 10, 8, 6, 5, 4 or as few as 3 rounds.

World championship professional fights are scheduled for 12 rounds of 3 minutes in duration with a 60-second interval. Amateur fights may be 2 or 3 minutes in duration and usually up to 5 rounds with 60-second intervals.

Fighters return to their nominated corner at the end of each round to refresh, repair and recover as they discuss tactics with their corner men or seconds, as they are sometimes referred to, between the rounds.

Over the years, I have heard street fighters comment that boxing is easier than fighting in the street. In my opinion, it is actually harder to fight when there are rules, and by comparison, a street fight is a piece of cake. My experience, having worked as a doorman since the age of 15, is that the thugs who bully and start trouble stand no chance against trained fighters, and that applies to boxing, kick boxing and MMA.

Officials

Three judges score the fight round by round. There is a timekeeper, a score master and a referee to supervise the fight and ensure the safety of the fighters. The referee ensures that the rules are observed at all times, has the authority to stop a fight, and instructs the judges regarding penalties.

Doctors attend both amateur and professional contests. In addition to an annual medical, there is a pre-fight medical examination for every contest. A doctor officiates at ringside, will advise the referee regarding the condition of fighters, and can indicate whether they are fit to continue. The referee can call the fight on the advice of the doctor, and in 50 years of watching boxing, I have never known a referee to ignore a doctor's opinion.

During professional fights, there must be a paramedic team inside the building and an ambulance waiting. A doctor must always be present, a neurosurgeon on call, and a hospital location identified to perform emergency surgery. Oxygen is required ringside for immediate use if required. Those are the minimum precautions at this time for professional fights as mandated by governing commissions in North America and Europe. These precautions were implemented following the evaluation of incidents that ended in serious injury or death.

Additional commissioners and assistants will supervise professional shows in strict accordance with the rules as per the governing body or commission.

Most shows have a master of ceremonies, and traditionally, glamorous round girls who get into the ring between rounds to remind spectators which round is coming up (see image at the end of this section).

We put on a show and the girl lost her nerve at the last second and would only stand in a corner.

Occasionally, fighters have been rescued by their chief second without the need for a doctor when the corner feels that the fighters' bravery exceeded their ability to continue.

Throwing their towel into the ring would signal an end to the fight. Sometimes this convention may be specifically forbidden in professional fight contracts but it seems to make little difference on the night.

I was chief second at a wrestling contest in Sweden; a super-fight. They take wrestling very seriously there, and, during the fight, my wrestler sustained a broken clavicle (collar bone). Both the fighter and referee were unaware of the situation. He was fighting the European champion at judo, and, despite the serious nature of the injury, he won. Because I could see the deformity from the ringside during the match,

I was ready to throw in the towel if he had deteriorated at any point.

I have never thrown the towel in for one of my fighters, but I considered throwing the towel in to save one opponent who was getting beaten very badly by my fighter. The youngster ended up outside the venue after the fight vomiting when we left. I think he had cracked ribs and a possible concussion. My fighter had heavy hands and I knew his opponent was taking too many shots, but the referee did not realize how much force the young man was enduring.

If you are to throw in the towel, stand on the apron and wave it, as it is more likely to be seen.

Weigh-ins

Weigh-ins for professional fights (and some amateur matches) take place the day prior to the fight as a safety precaution because of a direct correlation between dehydration and brain damage in fights.

Some boxing events, especially amateur boxing shows, arrange the weigh-in on the day of the fight, possibly to save money on hotel bills for out-of-town fighters and trainers. They may be unaware of the risks of not allowing athletes sufficient time to rehydrate before competing. They really should appreciate that weight loss, especially dramatic loss, may bring with it weakness and dehydration, with the associated possibility of greater risk of brain damage.

Making Weight

There is an art to making weight, and ideally fighters should be around 10 pounds above their fighting weight, smoothly dropping to the exact weight on the day. Good luck with that! Fighters can be way above and that is not unusual. I had two fighters drinking Mutant Weight Gain whilst trying to lose weight for fights last year and that caused a little confusion. You have to watch them like hawks.

Making weight is a miserable process. It's a tightrope between building strength, endurance, and technique whilst dieting and training down to the weight. Muscle weighs more than fat, and one problem is that young fighters are moving up in weight naturally as they develop, and there is little you can do.

I like fighters to be five pounds or so above with a week to go. The last bit can be lost by careful intake of water and food for a day or so, resting up to the weigh-in. We carry an electric scale and weigh daily at the same time as the actual weigh-in time for the fight for a couple of weeks prior to the fight. If the weigh-in is at 5 p.m., then the fighter is weighed at 5 p.m. every day.

I have known fighters so desperate to make weight that they scraped the sweat off their skin with old credit cards, sitting in saunas until they are cooked. Of course, this drains you and is a very bad idea. I sat in a sauna with Errol Christie in Coventry, and he was trying to make weight to fight a guy who knocked out his brother when he was amateur. He was out of shape and said the only thing he could do was KO the guy in the first round. He did. Errol was a superb amateur but may well have burnt out before becoming a professional fighter.

Trainers kneeling on their stomach to assist defecation, running or skipping - any way you look at it, losing weight on the day is very bad. These techniques impact on the fighter because they are using energy and can have a toxic effect on morale. It reflects badly on the trainer if the fighter fails on the scales.

Chinese diuretic teas work and can be vicious.

I have heard stories of MMA fighters having to remove blood, bag it, then replace it after the weigh-in.

Years ago in Sweden, I had a member came to my gym and collapse during training. It turned out he had donated blood that day, and I was lucky he did not end up in hospital. He was in a bad way.

Diet involves mostly lowering carb intake, eating regular small meals to suppress hunger, and sucking small ice cubes instead of drinking water. I knew a professional fighter so addicted to fries he would take one and rub it around his mouth, then throw the fry into the garbage intact.

I have known wrestlers who have eaten only jars of baby food to portion intake in a radical way. Diets that are so strict make the fighter's personality change, and I have seen guys behave in peculiar ways.

Conversely you have fighters moving up in weight who elect to wear their clothes at the weigh-in to close the gap because their opponents are on the limit whilst they may not be close. Perhaps they do not want to give their opponents any kind of psychological advantage.

I had a fighter and buddy come to me with the news that my fighter was over the weight by several pounds. I put my guy on a treadmill to run it off. It turned out that he was well under and I believe they misread the scale. It was a massive mistake made by me. Never take their word. Always weigh the fighter and have the scale checked if there is a discrepancy. I will never make that mistake again.

My fighters have always made weight. It's always tricky making weight. Some professional fighters have failed, electing not to accept a financial penalty or have lost a championship on the scales, negotiating to fight a lighter fighter and dispensing a monumental beating with a strength and weight advantage that they carried into the fight; I would never agree to that.

Always be present for the weigh in of both fighters and check the reading.

Never agree to work the corner for a fighter and put your club's name and reputation on the line, only to discover they did not train. I once worked the corner for a professional fighter who promised to do his weight training and conditioning independently. It transpired that he had not done any of the agreed training and had no force at all in his punches. It was a disaster, and I will never again assist a fighter who has not given 100 percent to the training. To his credit, he came and apologized to me in person. That fighter had absolutely no chance of winning which makes me wonder what the motivation was.

Exhibition Matches - Normally Amateur

Exactly as it sounds: two fighters in the ring to provide an exhibition of boxing with no decision at the end.

I never fought in one - I don't like them - and I would not advise anyone to agree to them.

Countless times I have seen trainers urging fighters of both sexes to really go for it - the opponent unaware of their intentions. Frankly, it's disgusting and can easily go badly wrong. Be very careful as the experience a fighter gains from an exhibition is not worth the risk. I have seen exhibitions with fighters of different weights in there, and guys who might fight in the future, being manipulated to do an exhibition to reveal their style and the dynamics that would present in a real fight for one coach's benefit. I refused every time, and I was asked many times. Bottom line: put the gloves on to fight.

Scoring – Professional

Judges award points for each round, with the winner receiving 10 points and the loser of the round receiving fewer than 10 points. To determine a winner based on points, the scores are totalled by the score master after the final round and announced by the MC. This is known as a "10-point must system" because the judge must award 10 points to the round winner.

The scorecard for each round is handed in at the end of that round, and the next round is judged only on what occurs in that specific round.

Judging and scoring is on a round-by-round basis. It is subjective and is based on effective aggression. All point deductions are done at the instructions of the referee. If judges see an infringement and the referee does not, the judges must ignore it.

Professional judges and referees receive training to reach a professional standard, then obtain experience moving towards championship fights and even world championship fights if they do an outstanding job. One bad decision could see them returning to the normal circuit, and there have been some serious mistakes over the years.

Judges may also be influenced by external factors. I believe the score in each round should be displayed in the stadium to motivate fighters.

In addition, a team of four cyber judges add their scores at the end to still give an exciting result. When the scores are combined with seven judges, the cyber judges can outvote a dubious score in the arena.

Scoring – Amateur

Amateur and Olympic boxing place greater emphasis on point scoring, to the extent that fighters have been trained for many years to present a narrower profile to avoid conceding points. This in turn has promoted flawed technique, which has gone around the world. The training, which is structured incorrectly, is therefore systemically flawed.

Amateur fighters may survive for years, winning national titles over and over by using styles developed to satisfy the scoring system. This has enabled fighters to score and yet to avoid being hit as a result of flawed stance. The fighters became so specialized that amateur boxing started to resemble birds pecking at each other.

Amateur fighters have been absolutely destroyed in light sparring at professional gyms. I have seen this myself - guys winning titles for years who are simply not equipped to fight properly. It an obscenity that this should have happened, and the regime who are entrenched are either too stubborn or too dumb to change.

Inevitably, interest waned in boxing, but the rules, safety requirements and bureaucracy powered ahead to a point where even the Olympic and amateur officials responsible eventually recognized the damage being done.

In an attempt to address the situation, the Olympic organization moved their scoring away from an electronic system that counted every peck. Unfortunately, judging at the last Olympics was so bad that it tarnished the entire Olympic boxing tournament, and questions regarding donations resulting in fighters winning have been raised.

At such tournaments, the red and blue corners receive the scores before the beginning of each round so they know their position.

As a direct result of both amateur and Olympic decisions, the public no longer has the same passion for amateur boxing, and responsibility rests squarely on the shoulders of the Olympic and national amateur boxing organizations.

This in turn, has had an effect on professional boxing since the pool of great fighters moving through is reduced. This is a serious problem. We need great amateurs, and it is fortunate that not all countries subscribe to the training. Golovkin and Lomachenko both had wonderful amateur careers and carried mass and acceleration into the professional ranks.

Old trainers, like myself, need to tie the arms of amateur fighters to their bodies and force them to punch from the legs rather than use just their arms. We restructure the way they punch and teach them to hit correctly.

The fundamental differences in leverage and technique that have crept into boxing prevent amateur fighters from moving and hitting with force after being trained at amateur clubs that teach the incorrect amateur stance and the associated flawed technique.

The Internet is riddled with "coaches" promoting a technique that is totally incorrect and not viable in real boxing.

Olympic and national coaches are not the best in the country. I would send the coach who trained the fighter from scratch to the national championships and to the Olympics with their fighter.

It's all part of the same flawed system that assumes that amateur and Olympic organizations automatically know best.

"It stops hurting when the check clears." -Sugar Ray Leonard

Differences Between Professional and Amateur Boxing

In terms of judging and points, there should be no differences, but there are.

The primary difference between amateur and professional boxing is simply that professional boxers are paid per fight and may be under contract to fight.

Of course, professional bouts are longer and may be extremely rough. However, there are a number of basic differences, which we have detailed, that harm the sport at the amateur level. I cannot think of a sport so radically different in the transition from amateur to professional. It's like tennis having different scoring and criteria.

Being a professional fighter is not a guarantee that you are good. The fact is, provided you make it through the medical, anyone can be a professional fighter, assuming you can find someone to pay you to fight. You are not going to last too long, but you would satisfy the criteria to say you were a professional.

I sparred with a lot of professional fighters, some highly ranked. The primary difference is they hit harder, absorb punches and keep on coming. The more skilled are really gifted.

As a youngster, I found that I was faster, but most professionals could take a really good shot and come back. Professional fighters hit harder, use more angles and pivot retaining balance. The difference is night and day.

Once you become a professional and start fighting, it is difficult to return to amateur boxing as amateur rules preclude this.

The medical for professional boxing normally involves a full examination, a brain scan and blood tests.

In some parts of the world, professional fighters are paid as little as $10 per round after traveling many hours and sleeping on floors. In North America, the rate can be as little as $100 per round for athletes starting on the long road as professional fighters. That is very little compensation for the discipline and dedication required and the risks and wear and tear are high.

Recently, cognitive tests have been suggested for amateur fighters to regularly assess cognitive ability for safety, and that is a great step. I am all for safety. This would be great in professional boxing as well.

I trained one professional who travelled to Uganda and won. In Uganda, amateur fight teams sometimes share one mouth guard to train and fight. He said that he was treated wonderfully there.

It is not uncommon for professional fighters to be given a certified cheque after the show. I knew one fighter who lost his cheque and could not understand why he was not given another.

Amateur boxers are not paid, but they are allowed to be sponsored and can compete in regional, national, international and Olympic competition.

The pool of talented amateur boxers has diminished massively as many youngsters gravitate to other sports at college. They smoothly transition to professional sports receiving huge financial incentives that boxers could only dream of.

Insurance for amateur boxers is through blanket policies covering gym activities such as sparring and competition. Such coverage is held by the organization or governing body and extended to participating clubs. Insurance for professional fighters is available for shows on a show by show basis and coverage varies. There are very few brokers in the U.S.. Insurance coverage for professional shows may vary due to the possibility of disruption by fans. The higher the risk, the higher the premium.

Head guards can be worn in amateur fights, although, thankfully, this is being phased out. Professional fighters use head guards to avoid cuts only during sparring. Head guards do not protect the brain inside the skull enough to be worn for that purpose. The protection afforded would be the same as donning an overcoat and stepping in front of a speeding truck.

Amateur fighters often wear singlets (vests). This is not done in professional boxing.

The Purse

The money that is won in professional boxing is referred to as the purse. In days gone by, the total purse was given to the winner. Now the purse is divided, and factors that determine the ratio may include but are not limited to the champion risking his belt, the popularity of the respective fighters, the amount of pay-per-view generated, the leverage a title holder has, and the desperation of a challenger to fight for a championship.

Dividing large purses seems inherently flawed since the incentive to win diminishes if you are picking up an astronomic amount to fight e.g., Alvarez vs. Mayweather. The fighter wins when he signs the contract, and the fight could be reduced to 12 rounds of sparring.

One contender in a championship fight bet heavily on the champion – his opponent. If he won, then he would have the comfort of the championship to make money. If he lost, then he would have his winnings to get by on. As it happened, he won.

The manager or trainer may deduct typically 30 percent. This equates to next to nothing in the early stages of a fighter's career. Later, however, if a fighter is extremely successful, the percentage might be renegotiated because often the fighter might feel that 30 percent is excessive for the trainer/manager.

In the early stages of a fighter's career, Sugarrays has never taken anything from the fighter's purse.

Rocky Marciano reportedly signed a contract giving his manager, Al Weil, 50 percent, and it has been suggested this was one of the primary reasons for his early retirement - along with his brutal training regime and a concern over attendance payments that he believed did not get fully shared.

Tough Man, White Collar Fights and Quasi-Charity Events

These are contests organized by gyms with fighters with nominal training, sometimes under modified rules with heavier gloves.

The funds generated may go entirely to a charity or organization that has been designated to benefit. Over the years, however, I have known of clubs that have taken huge donations and diverted the funds to support the commercial club and themselves. This is an utterly disgusting practice and is more common than the public thinks. It's easy to identify clubs that operate this way. Sometimes they have a charity as a separate entity, so the club itself is not accountable for funds once they are diverted their way.

I can confirm that 100 percent of all funds generated by our involvement as a gym have gone to the charity. Nothing, even out-of-pocket expenses, has ever been taken. We have not registered any charity to link to our gyms.

In order to be involved with any event organized by a third party, we would be looking for confirmation of exactly where the funds are going. If there are events on an annual basis, what happened to last year's funds?

These "charity" events can generate hundreds of thousands of dollars per show using the underprivileged or the abused as an excuse. Unfortunately, the funds may not reach the intended recipients, and that is unconscionable. Often, vast sums of money are left in accounts until the gym closes and the organizers pocket the lot. Alternatively, the property the gym is in is paid for and sold, and thus the funds are released.

Rivalries and Reputations

Professional fighters often stimulate interest in fights by creating the impression in the press, on TV and online, that they hate each other. Sometimes the rivalry is life-long and genuine, and things are said that cannot be forgotten. Often, however, it's simply expedient.

Professional fighters have the option to use the fight to address comments and personal issues, and there are many examples of such behaviour. Sometimes you see a fighter look to the referee to intervene on behalf of their opponent, e.g., Larry Holmes vs. Marvis Frazier. Not so common but a humane attempt by Larry Holmes, he never received the recognition he should have as a professional athlete, mostly due to his defeat of Ali and a couple of off-the-cuff comments. Make no mistake - he was a terrific athlete. Holmes's resting heart rate was reported to have been 30 beats per minute one hour before he fought Gerry Cooney.

More recently I have noticed a trend towards vindictive exchanges between fighters. There is a line that some fighters cross to enter areas that reflect badly on the sport. It is worth considering that many great fighters totally avoided such public statements.

Adrian Broner has made being detestable into an art form. The reality is that a lot of fighters go out of their way to look worse than they really are. I bet Adrian is a great guy who is just following his mentor Floyd Mayweather by stimulating notoriety with public disdain instead of punching power.

I knew one professional fighter who thrived on a reputation as a night clubbing party animal. The reality was that he was in bed by 10:30 every night and trained like a machine. You can't believe everything you read.

Now we see amateur youngsters trash talking each other, mimicking the professionals. I encourage our fighters to focus on training and, if asked, just say they will do their best.

Fighters would do well not to read Internet comments, as they can be corrosive. They are posted by trolls, gutless jerks who have no effect and just fade away if you ignore them. There was a great story about one in Newcastle, England who criticized a boxer, got tracked down, and was made to apologize in fear of his life.

Finding Fighters

As a trainer, I have found hundreds of fighters who want to train and don't want to fight and, conversely, fighters who want to fight and don't want to train.

The tough disciplined hungry fighters are out there. The challenge is finding them.

One interesting point is that, after 50 years, I still can't tell when a person walks in what kind of potential they may have at the reception. It is an amazing aspect of this sport, actually, that nobody can predict this, because there are so many factors that compose a fighter. I am reaching the conclusion that they find you.

After he retired from boxing, the great Archie Moore went to northern Canada in search of the abnormally large aboriginal people who lived there looking for a potentially great fighter.

I have had several heavyweights with potential; however, their personal issues meant they changed gyms more often than they brushed their teeth, and they could not even spell the word "integrity."

What defines how successful you can become is not how talented you are; it is simply how hard you are prepared to work. Isn't that true of everything in life?

Checkered histories and financial and personal problems can provide obstacles to success, and these issues can make everything so much more difficult. There is a point when some fighters are more trouble than they are worth.

Ali was the first man into the gym and the last to leave as a youngster.

They are out there. They just have to find you.

The secret is that you get out exactly what you put in.

Work harder than everyone else. Repeat every movement until it becomes a reflex action, until it's beyond thought. Strive to be perfect technically. Utilize force, but always with commitment to defence.

Constantly go back to the basics and strive to be the best at everything.

Repetition. Repetition. Repetition.

Rocky worked harder than anyone. Marciano used to go into seclusion at Grossinger's Catskill Resort. He trained perhaps harder than any fighter in history and watched comedy shows nightly to raise his morale and assist his recovery during his three-month legendarily brutal regime.

He was said to have run eight miles twice a day, but once an old man who was there at the time wrote on the Internet to contradict a sceptic and confirmed that sometimes he ran 14 miles.

Marciano had the disadvantage of short arms - the reach of a Malibu Barbie.

His trainer, Charlie Goldman, developed a deceptive crouching style that enabled Marciano to land devastating rights from the crouch. He held the title for four years and retired undefeated.

Several fighters commented on the difficulty of hitting him cleanly, including Archie Moore.

Asked if he could have beaten Ali, Marciano replied, "I'd be conceited if said I could, but I'd be lying if I said I couldn't."

Ali and Marciano made a movie depicting a fictitious fight between them, and several alternative endings were filmed. The ending used in the final version was determined by computer and showed Ali being knocked out in the 13th round. Ali later quipped that the computer must have been made in Alabama.

"Champions aren't made in gyms. Champions are made from something they have deep inside them—a desire, a dream, a vision. They have to have last-minute stamina, they have to be a little faster, they have to have the skill and the will. But the will must be stronger than the skill."
-Muhammad Ali

On the advice of his father, Muhammad Ali elected not to have his amateur trainer, who had taken him all the way to Olympic gold, as his professional trainer.

In the early years, Ali wanted Sugar Ray Robinson as his manager, but Robinson was still an active fighter.

His first professional trainer was Archie Moore, the hall of fame veteran and one of the greatest finishers of all time. Ali did not like the harsh training or washing dishes, so sadly, he fired Moore and moved on to Angelo Dundee, who was more of a corner man than a technical trainer.

Consequently, Ali's best performances were at the beginning of his professional career, when his movement and reflexes and skills were truly mesmerizing. He was a superb athlete in every sense and an extraordinary sports personality.

It has been said that Sonny Liston had so little regard for Ali that he did not even bother to train for their epic first fight on February 25, 1964.

Ali truly shook up the world to became the most recognized person on the planet.

Sadly, as Ali got older, his astonishing ability to absorb punishment became more and more of a feature both in training and in fights.

The punishment Ali took had a catastrophic effect on this wonderful athlete's health.

https://www.youtube.com/watch?v=OezriPEepZs

In considering Mayweather's achievements, the definition of a professional is earning money, and in that, he has proven to be outstanding. His greatest skill, however, is not his balance, timing or defence. Unfortunately, these are totally eclipsed by his microscopically detailed selection and rejection of credible opponents, causing some experts to suggest that he has been too selective to be considered an all-time great, despite his success.

I once had the pleasure of meeting Joe Frazier and talked to him for a little while on my own. He made a great impression on me, and I really liked him.

Joe was a wonderful man and, although he was very ill, I watched him get out of a wheelchair and walk into a boxing arena to a standing ovation - head high, Stetson on, looking great. He passed away not too long after, and I was extremely sad to learn of his death.

Ali and Frazier provided that special rivalry. Joe was cast as the villain, but that was never the case. Two superb athletes putting it all on the line and leaving an indelible mark on history.

Joe Frazier was a brave, tough, relentless fighter who won many fights despite not being able to jab. His arms were damaged in a childhood accident and left to heal on their own because of a lack of funds. The result was that they did not straighten; hence, his relentless hooking style.

"Fighting is a sport. If you're not humble, it's going to bring humbleness to you." -Iron Mike Tyson

Internet Instructors

There are literally hundreds of instructional boxing films on the Internet. The qualifications and ability of the instructors makes them sketchy, to say the least.

The sincerity and quality of some of the films suggests that the information is legitimate. However, these guys are often producing videos to validate themselves, clinging to the "credibility" of making films to bolster themselves as coaches with well-meant, but profoundly flawed instruction.

The unfortunate truth is that a lot of people eager to learn can be totally misled by such instruction. Be careful.

Obligations

As a fighter you have an obligation to do ALL the training required and give 100 percent.

As a trainer you are obliged to offer the best possible advice and commit 100 percent.

Make sure that your fighters understand that in asking to fight they are obliged to do the training.

How and Why

Trainers must teach effectively.

It is absolutely essential that fighters understand exactly HOW to throw a punch or execute a move.

Moreover, fighters must understand WHY.

That way, when fighter does something incorrectly, they understand the implications and recognize that they have made an error and can make an adjustment.

This is far better than barking an instruction and leaving it there.

Getting Involved in Boxing – Joining a Gym

Many people are hesitant to join boxing gyms because they are concerned they will be injured, and that's totally understandable.

A boxing gym is a tough place, and the training is exceptionally hard. Members new to the sport should not be injured at all while training, especially at the beginning. Boxing gyms can be wonderful places, and back in the day, parents sometimes left infants there for safety if they had to do something urgent. There you have the paradox: boxing gyms are safe places, full of the toughest people. I believe this is true of most fight gyms.

All training should be supervised. Sparring and competition should always be optional, and sparring should not occur until hours of drills on movement, punching and especially defence have all been mastered. If the fighter is not fit enough, they should not be sparring. There are no time outs in boxing.

It should be mandatory for all members who are sparring to wear safety equipment: head guards, mouth guards, chest shields (females), groin protection (optional).

Years ago, a peculiar guy came to the gym and brought with him a fully padded RedMan protective suit. His intention was to spar and not have to worry about getting hit at all. He did not make it past the reception.

Balancing this, it is amazing that boxing tends to attract high-functioning members from all walks of life, from millionaires to struggling students, and everything in between.

We had a lovely homeless guy join the gym from Ireland. He lived in Stanley Park, and his intention was to make a film about surviving on his wits whilst living under some bushes. Unfortunately, his plans were ruined by a pack of ruthless marauding raccoons. They stole everything he owned and we had to sort out some funds and food. He contacted his family and, vowing to return, went back to Ireland, never to be seen again.

Always take care whilst sparring. I have often seen fighters trying to arrange light sparring, then, when they have the measure of their opponent, they start to hit much harder. This is why all sparring should be supervised.

When I was senior trainer at a professional gym in Sweden, I met a truly sadistic son of a bitch who used sparring as a legal way to seriously hurt anyone he could. The man was about 40 years old, powerful, with skills, but deranged. He had knocked people's teeth out and just relished inflicting pain. I approached the owners of the gym to get rid of him, but was unsuccessful.

In a wrestling class during technical training, his partner gave him his arm. I heard the partner scream, and that was the end of his career. He had been a professional MMA fighter, and the sadist deliberately ruined his shoulder. I was in the room, and it was sickening.

He tried it with me during some training and I almost broke his jaw. I wish I'd left that guy in a fucking coma. Guys like that have no place in boxing gyms. He would have been eaten alive in other gyms. The guy survived in a combat gym, enjoying some protection from legal recourse.

I have trained in some very dangerous places, including Northern Ireland during the troubles, and, obviously, you come across amateur and professional fighters that hit harder than they should.

I have kicked guys out of the gym who were too selective about their sparring partners (men with youngsters, for example) but now and again genuine danger may lurk, so always be careful and do not hesitate to speak to the trainers about concerns immediately.

As a rule, I tell fighters to always meet force with force, and that way you are less likely to be absorbing serious punishment while the trainer decides when to intervene with an instruction to lighten things up.

While we are on the subject, all trainers should have full background checks to run amateur or professional gyms.

There are gyms that are not police-friendly, and prospective members should steer clear of them. Police often want to avoid criminal contact off duty, and any gym has a huge question mark over it, in my opinion, if the operators are uncomfortable having police officers training there.

Force with force is also a good idea since not all coaches at gyms can discern when a fighter is hitting too hard, or, for that matter, is in deep water. You have to protect yourself at all times.

Money Laundering

Some boxing gyms have been suspected of laundering money by claiming large income from drop-ins. To separate ourselves from those clubs, we have a no-drop-in policy, and we are a drug free facility. I have known the police to sit for weeks counting every member entering a gym to ascertain whether the number of customers including drop-ins could possibly equal that claimed by the club.

Over the years we have always operated ethically and professionally. There are a lot of gyms out there that could not say that.

During the recession in 2008, I refunded the full membership dues to all students who were suffering. They could still train at the gym. We needed money, but they needed it more.

Boxing gyms have a special warmth. The jokes and friendships are starkly contrasted with the massive effort required to train. This is true of most fight gyms, and it's just a given in boxing gyms, probably because they have been around for so very long. Every city should have a couple of great boxing gyms.

Fighting for Food

Whilst you could argue that all professional fighters fight for food, most have second jobs and could not survive on the income and frequency of fights.

During the Great Depression, amateur fighters competed for prizes that they could sell or exchange to obtain food. In the U.S.A., the thriving period of professional boxing after the 1930s and 1940s may well have been due to increased participation in the amateur ranks.

We are dependent on great amateur fighters to produce great professionals. Amateur boxing directly impacts professional boxing.

"When I was a young fellow I was knocked down plenty. I wanted to stay down, but I couldn't. I had to collect the two dollars for winning or go hungry. I had to get up. I was one of those hungry fighters. You could have hit me with a sledgehammer for five dollars. When you haven't eaten for two days you'll understand." -Jack Dempsey

Stillman's Gym

The legendary Stillman's Boxing Gym in New York City was known as a mecca for the best fighters on the planet and for keeping kids off the streets during the Depression (see image at the end of this section). In 1919, the two millionaire owners invited Louis Ingber, a former private detective, to manage the gym. Ingber's irascible personality and his skill as a boxing trainer brought fame to the gym, and people called him "Mr. Stillman" so often that he decided it was easier to change his name than to correct them.

Lou Stillman wore a gun at his waist and posted guards at the door to eject anyone who didn't pay the 25-cent admission fee to watch the boxers spar. Anyone caught stealing was barred for life. The gym was notoriously unsanitary and unhealthy – the floors reportedly went unwashed for years and smoking was allowed.

Some of the boxing legends who trained at Stillman's were Jack Dempsey, Georges Carpentier, Joe Louis and Rocky Marciano. Gene Tunney refused to train there because Stillman wouldn't open the windows to let out the smoke. Stillman has been quoted as saying, "The golden age of prizefighting was the age of bad food, bad air, bad sanitation, and no sunlight. I keep the place like this for the fighters' own good. If I clean it up, they'll catch a cold from the cleanliness."

This was by far the best boxing gym in the history of the sport. Gleason's and all other boxing gyms pale in comparison. There was one rusty shower, which was frozen in the winter. The heating did not go on till there was a foot of snow on the sidewalk. In the summer the shower would not work because kids broke the local hydrants.

You could see your heroes training and sparring in preparation for fights daily - no kidding. Virtually all the best fighters went there and absolutely every trainer.

Angelo Dundee was a bucket boy at Stillman's.

Billy Duffin

Experience and skills often slip away with trainers as they die, but sometimes the trainers of years gone by pass on treasured information. The great trainers of today sometimes do so, with none more generous than Freddie Roach.

As a youngster I was lucky to train with Billy Duffin in Coventry, a wonderful trainer. I remember him holding the mitts for me while a rubber hose was doing a jig secured to his arm by dirty bandage. He was tough as nails. The hose was used for transfusions. He was very unwell, but never complained; in fact, he rarely even mentioned it. Who would do that today? I think the boxing gym kept him alive.

Billy could easily have been cast in any Rocky Movie. Small in size, but a trainer of huge stature, he was respected - no, idolized -by the other coaches.

He had been present when Randolph Turpin was training for his first fight with Sugar Ray Robinson. Turpin knocked his brother out sparring, they brought him round, and then Turpin knocked him out again.

Turpin was a vicious fighter. He fought from a deep crouch, and Robinson had great trouble landing in his first fight.

Turpin always felt that his stoppage in the return fight when Robinson won back the title was premature. He was incredibly bitter about it because he was stopped on his feet, and that's not a great way for a champion to lose the title.

My opinion was that Turpin was in serious trouble against the best fighter on the planet. It was a good call.

https://www.youtube.com/watch?v=Z3npTVGLrCs

Billy had very many stories and was a wonderful man. When he died, it was difficult to adjust, and I never found another trainer like him.

He told me a story about a local doctor who, after enjoying hospitality at a Coventry show, was so drunk he tacked the top of a man's ear to his head with a stitch. The injury was only a little tear at the crease between ear and head, and the fighter was shocked and very unhappy about the temporary repair.

At one show, I was gloved and warming up. For some reason, I was on earlier than usual, which I loved as I could then watch the fights. Mostly I fought later. Anyway, a man popped his head in and said, "McAdam can go on after the interval."

Billy said, "Lads, get your bags." All our fighters picked up their bags immediately except me – I had gloves on.

The man said, "Billy, what are you doing?"

Billy said, "If Bob does not go on now, we are all going home."

I went on and won and never forgot that, even though I did not feel I merited the protest. Billy did.

Thirty years later, as chief second I told a guy we'd be out in 10 minutes, our allotted warm-up time, after he gave us just a one-minute final warm-up for the main event at an MMA show in the Black Box, Galway, Ireland.

Actually, I told the guy to go fuck himself as we would be taking the full ten minutes.

He said he was going to see the producer, came back, and said that would be fine. What were they going to do? It was the main event.

We won in forty seconds.

I thought of Billy and knew he'd have done exactly the same thing.

Billy Duffin was a superb trainer, and it was the little things. He would look at the skin of a fighter to see by the sheen if he was in shape or over the edge. If a fighter's skin was matt (without sheen) he reasoned they may have over-trained or need to rest.

He would often stand back and watch activity in the gym, only going over to give tips

He liked a joke, and I remember miles away from home at breakfast he was asking the locals about the location of the nearest swamp. He wanted a leech for a swelling on my eye following a clash of heads after a fight, and I was laughing right up until I realized he really wasn't joking. It put me right off my breakfast. Now I believe they are using them in hospitals. He was way ahead of his time.

Billy wore old worn clothes, like darned cardigans, old nylon tracksuit tops and flannel trousers. He didn't have a lot of money. I realize now that he knew he was very ill, yet he continued to train fighters, and the advice he gave was priceless.

So often the measure of a man is not how much money he has.

Nearly fifty years after he died I still remember him, ready to share a joke and pass on advice, a twinkle in his eye.

The boxing gym was at the back of the social club. I loved the gym. There was absolutely nothing of value in the gym but Billy, and he was priceless.

Through my years in boxing I have been privileged to meet some of the greatest ever - trainers, fighters and officials - but simply rubbing shoulders does not make you better. You have to learn as much as possible and hone your craft.

Money

Professional fighters can make huge amounts of money fighting in championships or defending championship titles at various weights. The vast majority of fighters, however, have to work in other jobs to make a living, whilst working through the rankings to attain the chance of a title. Very few fighters enjoy serious sponsorship or the comfort of financial stability on the way up. It's when fighters are at the top that the sponsors are queuing and not, ironically, when they really need help.

Professional boxing is a multi-million-dollar industry. There are a lot of people making a lot of money supported by public demand, but the fighters make next to nothing and often scrape to get by. It's really tough, and it is no surprise that a career in professional boxing is not as attractive as other sports.

However, there is no sport that defines a person more effectively than boxing.

Padded Records

I have known of professional fighters whose records are based purely on fighting "dumplings." Their objective is carefully to work towards a world title and cash in at that.

One story involved allegations that a former world champion was paid to assist in the manufacture of a fighter. As the story goes, there was an agreement that he'd go down in the third round. However, he was so upset at the younger fighter's genuine attempts to hurt him - even though the fix was in - that the ex-champ came out and flattened him in the in the third, got on the plane and went home. These, of course, are only allegations.

Fighters who claw their way to the top often lose their money quickly through poor investments, hangers-on and fast living. It is easy to forget what it took to win that title, to beat that fighter, how hungry you were and how much others want to take it away.

Sir Henry Cooper

As a youngster I did an exhibition of boxing at the town moor Newcastle, and Henry Cooper, former British Heavyweight Champion, attended as a V.I.P.

He arrived in a white Rolls, and one of our trainers said that Henry was an underwriter for Lloyd's of London. Years later, I read that he sold his three Lonsdale belts (each belt awarded for three British title defences) to help pay the debts incurred in a bad year for Lloyd's. Not everyone honored the obligation that year. In 1999, Henry Cooper was knighted - the first boxer ever. He definitely deserved the honour. He was a man of great integrity.

Years ago, I was listening to a live radio broadcast of the Hagler vs. Minter fight, and Henry Cooper was commentating and caught up in the fight. At one point, he said Hagler had opened up two "lovely cuts" over Minter's eyes. For just for a second, there was a glimpse of the true mindset of a professional fighter. When he realized what he had said, he apologized and said it was a very tough sport.

It was indeed a very tough sport. Cooper knocked down Cassius Clay (who later rejected his "slave name" to become Muhammad Ali) with his superb left hook during their 1963 non-title fight at Wembley Stadium. Clay's trainer, Angelo Dundee, then illegally used smelling salts to revive Clay, who was totally out of it.

Naturally left-handed, Cooper opted to lead with the left and deliver the powerful jab and superb hook in preference to being southpaw. Ali's astonishing powers of recovery and Henry's serious issue with cuts over the brow of each eye lost him the fight quickly, but not without Dundee's dubious assistance.

https://www.youtube.com/watch?v=Frn3rTj5DOY

It was truly an honor to meet Henry Cooper, an absolute gentleman and a great British fighter.

I would not have particularly wanted to meet Dundee.

Managers, Trainers and Promoters

Many life-long friendships and training relationships have dissolved in the caustic acrimony of financial disputes or betrayals caused by promises of greater opportunities made by other trainers, managers and promoters.

Professional fighters usually have a manager and a trainer, and sometimes they are one and the same. They work in conjunction with a promoter, whose role is to organize events. Fighters often have contractual relationships with trainers, managers and promotional organizations.

Most professional fighters have a pretty tough life. They train extremely hard, try to avoid injury, and hold down a job to keep food on the table. They hope that their trainer and manager will negotiate a safe route to a title and the rewards that follow. Fighters are often blinded by money and ill-equipped to deal with success. Getting there is a herculean task, and staying there is even harder.

Watching the Amateur Boxing Association Championships on TV in Britain, I heard Harry Carpenter, a commentator, disclose live to the nation that one of the fighters on the screen was registered as unemployed but had told Carpenter confidentially that he was working as a doorman on the side to make ends meet. That is actually a serious offence in the U.K.. Watch what you say. It's tough getting by - always has been, always will be.

Sugar Ray Robinson once berated a supporter for bad-mouthing Cus D'Amato. Robinson maintained that D'Amato's skillful management had generated huge low-risk pay days for Floyd Patterson. He admired this skill immensely because. during that same time, Robinson was involved in a series of very tough fights as a self-managed fighter.

The Muhammad Ali Boxing Reform Act, often referred to as the Ali Act, was enacted in 2000 by the U.S. Congress. Its main goals were to protect the rights and welfare of boxers, support state boxing commissions in the oversight of boxing, and increase sportsmanship and integrity in the sport. It was intended to eliminate the abuse of boxers through exploitation and the rigging of rankings and matches.

Promoters

A boxing promoter's primary objective is making money. Promoters should be treated with the same caution as an underfed 20-foot alligator. I have seen promoters forgo weigh-ins, lie about experience, assure fighters they are going to do well and manipulate fighters, all to their advantage.

At one unlicensed show, my fighter's opponent was the only fighter to weigh in, as I insisted so the opponent attended my gym and weighed in on Sugarrays scales.

Their interest can so easily be at a tangent to yours as a trainer or fighter.

Many fighters have close associations with promoters, which often results in acrimony.

Contracts

Professional fighters should have all contracts looked over by their own lawyer, not the promoter's or manager's lawyer, before signing. If the manager or promoter has nothing to hide, then there will be no problem with this.

Anything you agree to, especially in writing - and that applies to e-mails as well - can be legally binding.

Anything you amend verbally should be backed up in writing.

Keep a file with all legal documents and e-mails.

Protect yourself at all times, inside and outside the ring.

Do not be lured into taking ready cash to sign a contract without having it looked over by a lawyer.

If a contract needs to be adjusted, consult a lawyer for advice.

Perhaps you may recall how Don King rushed to attend the funeral of Jimmy Jacobs, co-manager of Mike Tyson, who died of leukemia in 1988 at 58 years of age. Besides paying his respects, King was laying a foundation for a future deal with the superstar. Mr. King is a poster boy for the less savoury side of the sport. He has promoted some amazing fights and provided an added dimension with his involvement. However, the controversy, legal disputes, bad publicity and beliefs that fighters have been taken advantage of all persist. He is very high profile, and it is just possible that there are worse under the radar. Predatory behaviour exists wherever there is money.

Too Bad You're Too Good

If you are too good, the public want to see you fight, but no one credible will fight you. This can dramatically impact on the earning potential of a fighter, and tempus fugit. This has always been a problem, and it forces fighters to take lesser opponents just to make money.

Fighters now are making strategic moves. Recently, two welterweight fighters moved up to middleweight to fight for large purses whilst realistically standing no chance. The towering advantage to this strategy was that, should they fail, they still retained their commercial value at welterweight. Since nobody expected the fighters to win, it would not affect their commercial value returning to their original weight.

The name of the game in professional boxing is making money. Both fighters had the balls to take the chance, but there is no luck in boxing and both got hurt badly. It might stop hurting when the cheque clears, but the damage can be permanent.

It was suggested that Sugar Ray Robinson moved to middleweight as no one was left to beat and make money at welterweight. He was just too good.

Gennady Golovkin has had real trouble finding willing legitimate opponents. The risk to their championship belt, future earnings and even health is just too great. This forces Golovkin to face lesser fighters, and time goes by. This has been going on for many years, and Golovkin is being deprived financially and historically and the public are not getting to see him attain his true potential.

The super fights still draw fantastic crowds, eager to observe the extreme tests their heroes are willing to take when we are lucky enough to witness genuine fights. Sometimes it is not even for the money.

Recording their place in history matters. It's a legacy thing.

"Boxing is the only sport you can get your brain shook, your money took and your name in the undertaker's book." -Joe Frazier
(Net worth at the end $100,000, but a National Treasure)

Sparring

Every trainer and fighter should read the following information about the potential effects of heavy sparring on cognitive ability.

Studies conducted in the U.S.A. confirm that fighters participating in heavy sparring are much more likely to be affected by diminished cognitive ability than fighters who have tough fights but avoid large amounts of heavy sparring.

It's a mathematical thing, heavy sparring. Three hard blows to the head a week, say 12 blows a month give or take, means you will be drooling like a bulldog faster than you can say "dementia."

Too much heavy sparring will result in damage. It's insidious, irreversible and accumulative.

Veteran trainers have noted that long after a damaged fighter has stopped boxing, the deterioration continues. Trainers should police sparring and limit heavy sparring to what is deemed absolutely necessary for fights.

Some fighters like James Toney elect to spar to get fit to fight. Those who do risk irreversible damage.

Bone-on-bone sparring takes its toll very quickly. Fighters' reflexes slow with age. You can get used to getting hit. It becomes addictive, and I have seen guys knocking lumps off each other in the gym for no reason. This is when fighters need trainers who care enough about them to do their job.

The pituitary gland is a small pea-sized gland hanging like a speed ball at the base of the brain. Its function is to determine hormone production. Damage to that gland can result in serious hormone issues, and this can be the cause of a number of serious problems. Some of James Toney's hormone levels are at a 70-year-old's level.

The long-term effects of heavy blows to the head should be of far greater concern than the death rate in boxing, which is considerably lower than the fatalities that result from horse riding, skiing, snowmobiling, soccer, football, and rugby.

Boxing carries a guarantee of cognitive damage if trainers fail to supervise heavy sparring, and these dangers are unquestionable. Because of this, we must take care. It is the paramount responsibility of trainers to ensure the safety of fighters, even from themselves. Over the years, a few top trainers have missed opportunities to fulfill that obligation, and unfortunately the results are there to be seen.

Larry Holmes was documented as stating that Ali took far too many heavy blows in sparring. We are simply not designed for such blows. Note how often the fighters with great defensive skills embedded in their fighting style are compos mentis and have long boxing careers.

The Unlimited Sparring System

Too many coaches opt for a system of natural selection, of survival of the fittest in their gyms.

This absolutely guarantees that many potentially promising fighters have walked in and staggered out long before they could really be evaluated. They have been beaten up by relatively unskilled guys who can do so by virtue of having been at the gym longer.

A lot of trainers favour this system, if only to ensure their guys get to move around, and justify it by claiming that they are testing the new guy. This just does not add up. There is nothing to test.

When getting ready for fights, these talentless coaches have their students do tons of sparring, I can reel off fighters from other clubs who I know are damaged permanently by the unlimited sparring system. Clubs adopting this form of training should be closed down.

Titles

Several professional fighters can simultaneously hold versions of titles at the same weight, all claiming to be the best and avoiding legitimate challengers.

The situation is getting worse and urgently needs to be addressed. You could argue that when enough money is on the table – it's on. That is not the case, however, because fighters hold on to a title and look for the best possible option, including fighters in lighter weight divisions.

There should be mandatory selection, and this could be done if an organization was formed that excluded any title holders or organization refusing to meet a mandatory challenger.

I think purses should be winner-take-virtually-all.

All shows should have money taken to support fighters' pensions.

I favour an imperative in winning. A friend of mine attended Mayweather vs. Alvarez and he said he'd seen more competitive sparring.

My point: they both earned huge money, so why do more than they had to?

Commentators

I have watched many fights and listened to commentators for years.

Sometimes I turn down the volume to watch the fight without the distraction of the commentary, as rarely do they reference the traps, the feints, the telegraphing and setting up opponents.

Recently, I watched a fight (Bradley vs. Rios) where massive tributes were poured on Teddy Atlas for the improvements in Bradley. Frankly, Teddy Atlas is a great guy - I have met him - but there was an obvious agenda. If there was improvement in Bradley, I did not see it in a fight where he was a huge favorite to win, anyway.

Bias

It's nauseating to hear commentators tiptoe through the mine field of hideous results, terrified they might upset the pay-per-view channel. They elect to protect their wages and future work and miserably fail to berate hideous decisions, offering, at most, a token gesture.

After one nauseating verdict, a PPV commentator justified the result by saying that although the winner did not actually win, the popular fighter got the decision, so in a sense it was okay. That's like giving the runner-up in a sprint the decision because he wore nice shorts.

Here we see the conflict of commentators who are paid by the PPV. show and dare not discuss what really occurred, lest they lose a job next month. Their integrity is instantly thrust into question.

It is ironic that commentators freely ridicule and criticize fighters so readily, dismissing their ability as they contend with vicious opponents. At the same time, the commentators consistently fail miserably to raise even a token objection to appallingly flawed career-changing decisions made by judges on the very shows they are covering. They are gutless sycophants.

Harold Lederman is often a lone voice, I feel, and the best judge on the planet, in my opinion.

Reg Gutteridge (RIP) and Jim Watt, Roy Jones, Harold Lederman and Sugar Ray Leonard are wonderful. Reg Gutteridge compared Hearns's beating Sugar Ray Leonard in the early rounds of their first fight to watching Bambi getting mugged. Sugar Ray Leonard later won by stoppage, one of the greatest fights I ever watched. It truly defined a champion's heart and was a great fight by both fighters enhanced by the commentary of Reg.

https://www.youtube.com/watch?v=k-_3CHKE6-M

Judging

Unfortunately, one of the worst aspects of professional boxing is the decisions by judges.

It's not easy to judge. It is a massive responsibility, since you hold the dreams and future prospects of athletes in your hands. You have to get it right every time, and effective aggression is subjective. There is simply no room for bias. You must be scrupulously fair and totally unaffected by outside forces.

Recently, we had a fighter climb off the floor in the first round to take the fight to his opponent. We had one professional judge, and he awarded the fight to our man as he clearly won the next four rounds. Another suspect amateur judge gave all rounds to his opponent. That was tough to take when the effort my fighter made was Herculean and it was for a championship. As
I said, there is a responsibility to get it right.

There have been many horrible decisions and Oscar De La Hoya vs. Felix Sturm in 2004 was one of them. De La Hoya accepted the belt in a truly jaw-dropping result to secure a super fight with Hopkins.

https://www.youtube.com/watch?v=Af0yR8GU6mQ

One solution could be cyber judges that give scores over the Internet, the judges at ringside also scoring, but theirs being displayed every round. The final result would be the aggregate of four cyber judges and three ringside judges. This would provide the transparency and excitement whilst being fair to all.

Effective Aggression

At amateur and professional shows, you have to pay to get in, and no one would pay to watch a defensive exhibition. It has to be competitive to be entertaining.

Fights are judged on effective aggression.

Two fighters can be perfectly matched, but a tighter defence in one can make for "a very tough day at the office," as Mike Tyson has said, for the other. Fighters obtain no points for a tight defence, but eventually they may end up vegetative without one.

Fighters with an effective defence have much longer careers. Fighters who rely on reflexes can shine brightly, but if they do not have the fundamental skills to fall back on, they will lose horribly in later years.

Roy Jones Jr. possessed blistering speed and cat-like reflexes to the extent that he did not always employ good defence because he could rely on the speed and reflexes. In later years, he proved vulnerable. Reflexes and speed are usually the first to go.

CESTUS VARIATIONS
AN ANCIENT BATTLE WRAPS

ELEVATED RING

ROUND RING

RING GIRL

STILLMANS GYM
NEW YORK GYM OF LOU STILLMAN, A LEGENDARY BOXING TRAINER

OLYMPIC BOXING RING

FIRST PUNCHING BAG
GUARDED BY BARN DOG

KRONK GYM
DETROIT BOXING GYM ONCE LED BY LEGENDARY TRAINER EMANUEL STEWARD

Training & Technique

Past & Present

Instruction

Training in boxing gyms is legendarily tough.

Boxers rarely, if ever, go to other kinds of gyms to get ready to fight. However, over the years, there have been thousands of athletes who have come to or been sent by their coaches to get conditioned in boxing gyms to increase their performance in their own sports.

It is ironic that boxers are quite often the best conditioned athletes in any city. They often compete at the highest level imaginable, but without payment.

We had an NFL player research the gym, fly in, and shock his club into re-signing him for millions of dollars. He was a great guy, and we were sorry to see him go.

In This Section

The objective is to make every fighter as effective as possible. Therefore, we have to part company with amateur training and technique immediately.

We address warming-up in the gym and for fights, movement, balance, distance, timing, leverage, defence, and punching individually and then in combination.

Over the years, I have developed methods and equipment for fast-tracking movement and coordination.

Boxing is a synergy of will and skill. It involves timing and coordination. It is a combination of fluid and sometimes explosive movement with endurance, balance, leverage, timing, and will. It requires dedication, discipline and bravery.

The ability to move and punch cannot be underestimated.

Youngsters are used to intuitive computers with instant results, the hard work having been done in the background by programmers.

Unfortunately, boxing demands application, and patience. Although some master these qualities. faster than others, all must learn to move correctly because that is absolutely fundamental to everything that follows.

The guys and girls who pick it up fast are not necessarily the best in the long term. It is the students who persist, who are willing to work - and work hard - that can turn out to be the best. The key is repetition.

An effective stance retaining balance may take weeks or even months, but this is the foundation of everything to follow.

Over the years, we have had many students drop out as they did not have the resolve to work and perfect this basic requirement. I have trained guys with existing bad habits who have taken great offence in being told they had to modify their stance or start again.

I have known several older trainers who forbid punching for six months. My view is that it takes as long as it takes.

Trainers who move prematurely beyond basic requirements fail to do their job. We have found that some trainers want to create a rapport with students and bypass the fundamental training, leaving it for others to sort out later and taking the students to the fun of punching prematurely. We have let that quality of trainer go, as they make the work harder for the real trainers.

The reason we examine training and technique from the past is that great skills have often been lost. The belief that only techniques used today apply and are cutting edge is simply flawed.

Watching film of Sam Langford, we noticed that he placed his hand on his opponent's bicep in the middle of the ring. I tested what he had done and discovered that the opponent could not throw a punch because the leverage was against him. It was deceptively simple but incredibly effective and never used.

We look at everything to find anything of use now. No one ever lost a fight by being too good.

Warm-up

The warm-up is a low-impact opportunity to get the whole body working in order to avoid injury, build strength, and achieve conditioning prior to boxing training.

Our warm-up incorporates cardio, strength, endurance and functional elements. It is miserably tough, but you work gradually, increasing the number of reps and, in time, the number of circuits. Because the warm-up is tough, competitive fighters can be monitored and their exact level of fitness easily ascertained, astonishingly as others are training beside them.

Tip: There are a lot of fighters out there who, given the chance, may skip the warm-up or coast through. This is why a trainer needs to be present. Competitive fighters do not always have the resolve to complete the work required on their own, especially if they do not like training and conditioning. They often crave recognition for their efforts all the time, and the unobserved training just does not get done. Fighters get injured if the warm up is not thorough.

Consequently, most will do it as long as they are being observed and commended for their efforts.

Ideally, you want the fighters who get up at 5.30 a.m. and put on a toque and do their roadwork, strength training and conditioning on their own without constant praise. Those are rarer than hens' teeth, but they are the guys who make it all the way.

Our warm-up involves a Tabata-timed circuit using weights, ropes, chains, floor exercises and cardio.

You can buy the Sugarrays timer with Boxing, Bag and Tabata functions.

Chains

Weight training with chains greatly improves explosive endurance. Because of the net demand for oxygen and the need to continue the exercise over time, it may be prudent to have a medical since there is a massive demand on the cardiovascular system. Chain training is so tough we have to start off with very low reps.

Our fighters can currently win a free year at the gym if they can complete four sets of 50 clean press and squat. We are looking for a very clean exercise with a 30-second rest between sets. The chain training techniques are pretty much unique to us, while other gyms will have their own protocol to assist the fighters to warm up, build up strength and endurance. Who knows whose approach is best?

Circuits

Sugarrays incorporates body weight exercises, climbing ropes, chins, dips, as well as push-ups, jumping bands, and straddling tires. By combining explosive training, endurance, strength and cardio over time, we can train different levels of athlete all at the same time, and they will all see improvement at their respective levels.

Ropes

We use rope climbing to strengthen hands, wrists, shoulders, core and backs. The ropes provide awesome functional training. Chris Eubank climbed a rope to build his strength and endurance and to determine how close he was to being ready to fight. I met him many years ago as I was sponsoring a meeting for the ABA in the U.K., and at that time he was at the peak of his powers and immensely strong.

Back in the day, rope climbing was an Olympic discipline, and men could climb 20 feet in three seconds, arms only. That's as fast as a squirrel.

Our ropes are 15 to 20 feet in height and are climbing ropes of Manila 2" double secured at the ceiling. I pair the ropes so the option exists to climb two ropes with one hand on each rope. As you get fitter, climb from a seated position on the floor and try to climb up and down multiple times without touching the floor.

To avoid rotator damage, we do not use battle rope training

Weights

Amongst a lot of trainers, weights, and in particular heavy weights, are frowned upon.

All Sugarrays gyms have weights, and we strongly advocate using them, especially in circuits. Weight training is a great way to build strength and explosive endurance.

We need to ensure our fighters are as strong as full-time manual workers. The weight training that we advocate will compensate, and has the advantage that we can target exactly the muscles required for boxing.

Weight training programmes can be brutal, and it is a good idea to keep the puke bucket handy for the first couple of sessions.

Weights are great for mental strength as it takes great resolve to keep going and maintain form.

Safety

Heavy weights have a small margin for error. If you do choose to use heavy weights, warm up. You must employ perfect safe technique and gradually build up. Wear a weight belt, and have a spotter to assist you.

Weighing Up Weights

You have to be careful using weights as it adds weight to the fighter (muscle is heavy). Boxing employs functional training rather than cosmetic body building. Developing heavy muscle is useless without endurance, and it can slow you down badly. Further, the extra weight can place you in a heavier weight division and firmly at a disadvantage.

If bodybuilding was great for boxing, surely the best fighters would be bodybuilders. They are not, so it suggests heavy weight training, and especially bodybuilding, are of no use to fighters.

I rarely go as high as body weight in training fighters.

Bodyweight Exercises

There are some massive advantages in using your own bodyweight. It's cheap, effective and unlikely to result in serious injury.

You can obtain clear indications of improvement through the reps you can achieve. It's functional and you do not require rooms full of gym equipment.

Some possibilities:

-Push-ups
-Crunches
-Ab exercises
-Burpees
-Squats
-Chins
-Dips
-Dorsal lifts
-Jumping
-Straddling tractor tire
-Lunges

Skipping

Every boxer should skip, but not all boxers can. Injury is the primary reason.

Skipping is a skill that, health permitting, you should acquire. Persevere. It takes practice.

We have a rower and an exercise bike in case students get shin splints or have knee problems, skipping has the disadvantage that it is high impact.

Skipping is great for strength, coordination and conditioning.

We do three-minute rounds - an eternity when one first starts - then 30 seconds of push-ups with no rest period. As you get fitter, skip 15 seconds fast, then 15 really fast, alternating for the 3 minutes. Our fight team does 10 rounds. Our circuit involves a short sprint of 50 seconds skipping.

There are multiple benefits to skipping:

-Shoulder strength
-Coordination
-Leg strength
-Cardiovascular fitness
-Discipline: when you have to keep your form and relax and your muscles are screaming to stop.

You box on the balls of the feet, and skipping promotes strength in exactly the muscles you need to strengthen.

There is a huge element of discipline in skipping fast and maintaining form whilst your muscles are screaming "stop," and that's what boxing is all about.

At a point in the future, once you get the hang of skipping, you will be able to relax. When you first begin, that may sound very unlikely, but you will.

Other skills crossing, doubling will follow. There are different exercises and drills which can be practiced. One extra added benefit is that you are unlikely to get run over.

I favour a weighted handle and heavier plastic rope. The speed ropes make it a little too easy, but they are fun to switch up for exceptional speed sometimes.

I once skipped for five hours for charity.

Manny Pacquiao skips at a crazy rate for long periods of time, I am told.

Running (Roadwork)

There is a road outside your house. Make a route, make it safe, and include as many hills as you can. You must make sure you can be seen day or night.

Run three times a week, build up and run hard for an hour each time, five days out of seven if you are professional.

Towards a fight, sprint on a track if you have access, or sprint lamp posts or a measured distance on land or beach.

Real running, especially over hills or mountainous terrain, or sprinting on beaches and dunes really is superior to treadmills as you are moving your body weight. Treadmills are a distant second.

If they cannot run for any reason, fighters have put in the hours, by swimming, hiking, cycling, rowing, and still made the grade.

Consider running with a brick in each hand, or weights.

I trained a Canadian football star who had four surgeries on each knee. It was bone-on-bone agony. I took him hiking and snowshoeing to get fit. It had to be very hard work, but low impact. He made it back into the CFL. You have to find a way. If he could do it, you can too.

Most fighters run averagely well but are great on hills, stairs or mountains.

Avoid running downhill for long periods as it is very bad on your knees.

Overtraining

It is the responsibility of trainers to ensure that fighters perform at their full potential. Some fighters have to be strictly monitored as the obvious danger of overtraining is that "You can leave it in the gym."

Making weight may see fighters training hard just before the fight, when careful diet and water intake would be the ideal method for the last few pounds. Eating a good meal and rehydration offer quick recovery, compared to trying to recover from physical training to lose the weight the day before the fight. Training off the pounds is not a great idea physically or psychologically.

Puke Buckets

All our gyms have puke buckets close to the warm-up area. They are big and intended to be readily available and on quick release. You use it - you clean it.

Most often, the net demand for blood means there is less for the stomach. This triggers nausea, which, in turn, may make a fighter vomit.

Obviously, in the early training, we do not push the fighters too hard; however, there may be the odd one that is queasy.

A very cold wet towel or ice pack - we use Ziploc bags - on the back of the neck, sitting down on the ground or even lying down is recommended. You will get over this quickly and forget what is a nasty experience but not so uncommon.

Cross Training

Boxing offers strength, conditioning and skill.

I believe that pure cross training gyms have an inherent flaw: if you are increasing weight, reps and duration, something has got to give eventually, and its likely to be you. Further, it is expensive and you do not obtain a skill as you do with boxing. Recently we have seen a large return to boxing from cross training.

Time

The world has changed, and youngsters are used to intuitive computers, instant access and immediate skills. In the background, someone else is doing the programming and creating the product.

If only boxing were like that! It's not; it takes time. You need to pay your dues, work, and earn your skill.

Stance and Hand Position Orthodox (Reverse for Southpaw)

To adopt a boxing stance:

1. Stand with feet shoulder-width apart.
2. Step forward with left (orthodox) or right (southpaw).
3. Rotate front and back feet slightly (2 o'clock works to present a better angle to opponent).

Tip: With every centimetre your rear foot is moved too far behind your buttocks or your front foot too far forward, you will have less explosive movement and punching power. Consequently, excellent stance is absolutely essential.

Keeping feet at shoulder width ensures stability and gives the ability to punch correctly with force.

With feet in line, the back foot has to rotate. This is totally wrong, you end up unstable, and you can't move. Therefore, your own footwork restricts your landing punches.

Understanding Balance

Move into your stance. Your feet should be shoulder-width apart. Sway side to side. Bend at the knees. Touch the floor if you are comfortable. Move forward, front foot first, and backwards side to side, outer foot in the direction of movement first.

Never have your chin in front of your front knee.

Don't lean over to the left or right.

Don't lean forward or back from the waist.

Do not bring feet parallel or together when moving.

Utterly fundamental, balance may be considered the keystone of fighting. Balance enables a fighter to hit and keep hitting. Move or be forced out of balance, and the ability to hit is seriously diminished.

Look for opponents bringing their feet parallel as they move, and time attacks to coincide with this.

The narrow in-line stance adopted by amateur fighters brings with it instability, and that can be exposed.

There are one-off punches that carry a kind of all-or-nothing commitment, but a trainer will generally position the fighter's head in a protected zone: e.g., Martinez vs. Williams 2. where Martinez is not even looking at Williams.

Exercise to Demonstrate Balance

To demonstrate just how important balance is, adopt your standard boxing stance then:

Lean forward and see how it takes your leverage to punch and leaves

you exposed to punches.
Return to your normal stance.
Lean back to see again you cannot punch.
Return to your normal stance.
Lean to the left and right, and you cannot punch.

The reason for this is you have moved your centre of gravity. Sure, you can try to punch, but not with any real force and certainly not repeatedly, so you are very vulnerable.

Further, a lack of balance exposes your defence, as you cannot counter attack with any conviction.

There are some rules in boxing to keep you in balance:
1. Keep your chin behind your front knee.
2. Never bring your feet parallel.
3. Never cross your legs moving left or right. Move with the outer leg first, left or right.

Trainers of fighters all over the world have to ensure students appreciate how essential balance is at the very beginning to enable the transfer of weight, movement and maintain defence.

Very very slight bend of the knees.

Basic Training Movement on Rail and Rope or Line

Movement on rail and rope:
-Your stance as you stand should have a 50/50 even distribution of weight on ball of each foot.
-Moving forward, place 100 percent pressure on the back foot.
-Moving backward, place 100 percent pressure on the front foot.

Heel of back foot strokes the training rail. Toe of front foot strokes the rail.

Tip: To start with, step, step, step. Later, stay in contact with the ground and glide, glide, glide.

The closer you are in contact with the ground, the readier you are to punch.

Tip: Keep the front toe pointed slightly down. That prevents telegraphing your intention to move and ensures you remain close to contact with the ground.

When the ball of the front foot is on the ground, the back foot must move forward exactly the same distance to return the stance to the initial position. Position A and position B are identical. The feet move at shoulder width.

Tip: To assist students, I sometimes use a metronome, and it really helps. The beat can be slowed to a comfortable rate, and it has the benefit of stopping students from racing ahead and moving too quickly. I have both manual and electric metronomes, and they are very useful to slow down students and coordinate feet, and then feet and hands. Sometimes students race away and begin to move out of sync. The metronome can be a constant reminder of timing, which can be increased as the fighter becomes more comfortable and competent.

Muscles have to get used to this new movement. You must be coordinated.

Tip: A common problem is leaving the rear foot too far behind or failing to step in at all. The result is that you are straddling space.

As well as drills and shadow boxing, we use a large tire and strengthen the legs jumping a to b and b to a in three-minute rounds, but not hitting the tire with a bar as this can cause repetitive injury to the spine or kill somebody in the gym if you let go of the bar or sledge hammer.

Tip: Students leaving the back foot behind can have both feet connected by a rubber strap at the ankles. These can be bought from most fitness equipment stores and are cheap.

How important is it to master this basic movement?

It is so important that old-time coaches are happy to work on the basic movement for as long as it takes. People vary, and it takes time to learn a skill. This fundamental movement is off the scale of important.

Everything will be based on this: all advanced punching, pivoting, shifting, feinting, changing levels, in-fighting, alternative defences, everything.

Drills

Once the student has perfected moving in a straight line, we start doing drills to reinforce the fact that the stance and balance must be retained no matter what.

Later, we will tell students never to move back in a straight line. Their opponent will force them on to the ropes at the same time, the opponent gains momentum, and its only one or two steps till they hit the ropes.

At this point, I normally have students lean back again, lean forward to the left again and the right again to illustrate how doing so deprives the fighter of the ability to punch effectively by virtue of the fact that their centre of gravity moves, and this is fundamental to leverage.

I pair fighters and have them move as mirror images in a square dance.

```
                Forward
To the right           To the left
                Back
```

As they move individually around the ring, the trainer must ensure the fighters maintain their stance.

-Keep your chin behind your front knee.
-Never bring feet parallel.
-Never step forward crossing legs (except shifting to follow).
-Never cross legs moving left or right - ever.

Tip: Later, fighters must move around each other. Nine times out of ten (the ratio of orthodox to southpaw) orthodox fighters move to the right away from the power hand; however, the left hook and powerful jabs may present a hazard. Occasionally, the force of the puncher's hook is such an issue a fighter may move to the left (Ali vs. Liston 1).

Making a Fist

You won't last long with clenched fists.

A fighter's hands are normally open and relaxed inside the gloves. You will use too much energy if they are clenched, so only make a fist as you commit to punch. When punching, tighten the fist just before you make contact with index and second knuckle.

Tips: If you wiggle your fingers inside gloves, it's impossible the be tense.

Tension slows you down and burns up energy you could use to punch. Tension prevents the efficient exchange of oxygen and carbon dioxide in the muscles. Tension slows, and so you get more tense, and you slow even more.

The Ability to Relax

Every trainer has had to implore a student to relax. The problem is that the ability to relax is the reward of perseverance, and that involves time.

For example, skipping in the early stages whilst tense is an ordeal. As the fighter begins to relax with time, they become as one with the rope and the exercise becomes fluid; even during bursts of flat-out speed.

Tension is your enemy.

Tension burns energy.

Tension slows you down.

Tension gets you hit, and that creates more tension.

Tension begets tension.

Trainers have to evaluate the fighters' punches, movement and defence. If there are signs of tension, fighters need more time and practice.

We are asking fighters to perform unfamiliar moves, to enter a hostile environment, to compete against skilled adversaries. It is going to take time to relax.

Take any nerves, convert to speed, and give it back to the opponent

REPETITION, REPETITION, REPETITION TO RELAX.

Flawed Rotation

The twisting of ankles came from generations of amateur coaches insisting that fighters can make themselves less of a target by standing with their feet almost in line to avoid conceding points in a point orientated system.

This instantly deprived fighters of the ability to throw a right and land it, creating fighters with poor balance and therefore less leverage whilst forcing rotation of ankles.

To this day, the narrow lines employed in such gyms and on training videos automatically produce a narrow stance and from that second students are doomed by everything the coach instructs. It is manifestly flawed systemic nonsense. Pretty much all amateur coaches advocate twisting on the hook and right cross. It simply does not exist in real boxing, so they are all wrong. Advocating twisting instantly restricts movement and leverage, critically takes time and can result in imbalance if the fighter misses.

Anecdotally, you just do not see this in professional boxing, and none of the best fighters on the planet use this technique. The worry is that amateur coaches advocating this simply do not understand the necessity for speed and the need to land punches with force and have the ability move immediately.

I have no time for such coaches and frankly consider them imbeciles.

I am not saying I am right and they are wrong. I am saying I am absolutely right and they are definitely wrong.

They have got away with this and it has been recycled for generations; yet, watching professional fighters, you never see this movement.

A Darwinian moment, a manifestly flawed technique surviving through ignorance in an organization that is closed and intent on perpetuating this garbage through a flawed training system that is compulsory. Everything that's wrong with amateur boxing can be seen in this issue.

Because it looks like the coaches know what they are doing, it ticks a huge box. These coaches stay firmly in amateur boxing, and many produce videos, advise MMA, and on it goes - generations of flawed instructors advocating flawed technique.

To illustrate how crazy it is, it's impossible for amateur fighters to move forward throwing a left, right and hook combination if they twist their ankles. It cannot be right and never was.

A conveyor belt of training in amateur boxing ensures the next generation are primed and ready to go, inexorably moving forward, whilst paradoxically their students can't move at all in real life.

The Jab

Breathing:

-It's easy. Exhale as you punch.

-Breathe out through your mouth and in through your nose. If its blocked, then in through your mouth as well.

-Don't hold your breath.

Once correct movement and hand position are established, it is time to coordinate punching.

1.The First Punch - Learning to Jab

Initial technique is pretty straightforward:

-Keeping your hands in defensive position, step forward with your left foot (about one foot-length).

-Step back, returning to the original position, and repeat until comfortable.

2. Get used to that simple movement: stepping forward, stepping back.

3. Now, from the defensive position, the left arm extends from the shoulder.

-This is done slowly at first, but must be executed at blistering speed when sparring, boxing or hitting mitts and bag.

-As the arm straightens, the fist tightens in the glove.

-As the fist connects, punching through the target, the left shoulder touches your chin.

Keep eyes on your opponent; you should be exhaling as you punch.

Keep your chin down to protect your throat and stop your head and neck being snapped back should you be hit.

At this stage, you may decide to advance by stepping in with the rear foot (about one foot-length).

OR

Simply step back with your front foot to the original position.

Either way, the jabbing arm must return to the original defensive position at the same speed as the punch was thrown.

The front foot does not move anything like as far as the arm however the coordination of hand and foot must result in the foot landing on the ground as the punch connects.

Step in first then punch, you get hit.
Step in after the punch, it will not land.

As you perfect this movement, add a slight rotation of the torso to increase length and mass in the punch and add to defense by moving the right hand slightly a half inch across the face.

Force in Your Jab

The maximum force to jab is derived by the forward transfer of mass provided by the drive from the back leg.

Over the years, I have come to appreciate that possessing a vicious jab is a massive asset, and further that the return of the jabbing arm instantly to its defensive position is equally important.

Never throw a slow jab even when tired because you will be horribly exposed; the counter could be devastating. Further, gradual slowing of punches helps your opponent time you for a counter.

As your coordination becomes better, your torso rotates to the right, and extra mass and reach are derived from this.

Never jab out of range. In a genuine attack, falling short leaves you horribly exposed and telegraphs your intention.

You have to understand and appreciate distance. An inch too far away means you have to bridge the gap or you will fall short. Waiting to punch often means you will get punched.

Tip: A slow or hesitant jab is catastrophically bad. In the later stages of a fight it is essential, if you are getting tired, to cut down on the number of punches if you have to, but never reduce the quality. Feint more, but never have your opponent feel they can ignore your offence/defence. The quality must always be there until the final bell.

If you are tired, hurt, or not sure what to do, jab. It puts the greatest distance between you and your opponent. It requires timing, understanding distance, leverage, and imparting mass. You have to practice your jab.

Boxers jab to gauge distance, as a primary attack, to defend an attack, to break down an opponent's defence by forcing them to move their arms to defend the body or head, to buy time by stopping an attack, and to frustrate and to feint an opponent into a vulnerable position. A jab at the same time as an opponent's attack may frustrate a faster puncher by punching with the puncher.

It may be used to prevent an attack from an opponent by pre-empting an attack and to create a gap to land the right hand or initiate combinations.

Watch Golovkin dismantle Lemieux with his jab.

https://www.youtube.com/watch?v=9UazwqHspYg

Train hard, throw thousands, build up your shoulder and step in to transfer mass and truly damage your opponent.

You can sit down on the jab and parry and jab, causing your opponent to sustain a serious blow using their momentum against them.

Mayweather has a superb jab. De La Hoya angled his body to jab up to the extent that fighters complained of whiplash.

Ali utilized a flicking fast jab and alternated this with a vicious jab, sometimes corkscrewing his fist to try to cut his opponent, Ali reinvented that punch as it had been documented many years earlier.

Golovkin pulverized opponents with a solid brutal jab, knocking opponents down.

Larry Homes possessed a brutal jab.

When a jab is thrown, there should be a subtle movement of the right hand (a half inch across the face). To reduce the target area of the jabber's head to next to nothing, the fighter must remember to keep his chin down. The jabbing shoulder should end up protecting the chin, and the hand should be face down, landing with the index and second finger knuckles.

The fighter may elect to step in, transferring mass, sit down on the punch to use the opponent's momentum, or throw the jab (stick) and move.

When the jab is setting up other attacks or disrupting an opponent, it can be referred to as touching an opponent.

Not all fighters use a classic jab. There are exceptions to every rule. Joe Frazier, Rocky Marciano and Jersey Joe Walcott touched, and to an extent Mike Tyson fought early on without the jab as the primary weapon, using lateral movement to capitalize on an opponent's attack. There are many more.

Some fighters prefer to extend their jabbing hand to create distance and blind opponents to their right hands.

I always try to encourage a fighter to learn to jab first; in fact, not just jab, but to strive to have the best in the gym.

A good jab can win a lot of fights and will always beat a street fighter's wild swings. It must be accurate and not telegraphed, either by pulling back the hand to punch or by facial expression. Do not step in before you punch. Try to punch through the target eight inches.

Remember that the first punch often misses, so your second jab should be as good or better than the first. So often when fighters first get into a ring, the distance of a real opponent is greater than all sparring opponents, so initial punches (often a jab) miss. You may have to step in again with an even better jab. Don't do that pathetic half-second jab with no power; that's the one that lands.

Practice on a light bag (but not so light that you hyperextend, injuring your elbow), hitting it as it returns, 50 times per set. Build up your shoulder strength and work on the mitts, throwing one, two and three jabs.

Circling an opponent is less effective whilst jabbing, so try to step in, ideally orthodox to orthodox, with the front leg moving towards the groin.

Southpaw to orthodox, it becomes a battle to gain the outer foot advantage. Then you are able to land a power straight right or left.

Common Issues:
Fighters jab low on the bag. Vary the height of your jab for sure, but keep it real and hit at true head height. Then hit lower to simulate a drop in opponent's level. Place target markers on the bag. Be accurate and strike cleanly. Some bags have printed targets.

Be disciplined and step in and step or pivot away with your hands up.

Make sure your hand returns fast and does not drop on the way out or upon return. The latter cost Joe Louis dearly against Max Schmeling, who stated he had seen something that made him think he could win prior to the fight. Louis lost by KO, made an adjustment to his jab, and ultimately reigned as world champion for almost 12 years.

https://www.youtube.com/watch?v=lihT_ewxVko

https://www.youtube.com/watch?v=6BLGdFQPh8c

I believe Joe Louis was so desperate to fight for the world title that Mike Jacobs, his manager, agreed to give James J. Braddock 10 percent of Louis's earnings on future fights, if Braddock gave him a chance to fight for it before Max Schmeling.

Ensure punches are thrown from the defensive position and hands return immediately to that position to avoid telegraphing and maintain the best defence possible.

At this stage, it's a great idea to stop students from making faces, pursing lips and other mannerisms prior to punching.

Always consider defence, and make every punch technically perfect.

So now we have an extraordinarily valuable skill: coordinated movement and punching.

Tip: The movement of feet and hands must be synchronized, but the feet move a much smaller distance than the hands and arms, and therefore the hands and arms must move very quickly.

If you are George Foreman, then your arm may be enough to impart mass. If not, maximum force is derived utilizing the drive from the back leg. By converting mass, not just of the arm but of the entire body by punching and stepping in simultaneously, you are now punching with your body weight. It takes just a small amount of effort to hit so much harder. If you have good timing, then you can combine the mass of your opponent coming in to land a devastating blow.

Work on this. A great jab is a huge step towards being a great fighter.

Our advanced fighters use a variety of jabs to different areas.

Shifting Jab:

As the jab is thrown, the right leg moves forward, offering an opportunity to check hook with the right whilst enjoying a degree of safety to the left of the opponent as you are effectively moving past your opponent (Willie Pep).

Power Jab whilst leaning over to the right:

This can be very effective and offers great safety hitting to head or body (Sam Langford, Pep etc.).

Points to remember:

-$F=ma$ through the target

-Stay relaxed.

-Punch fast.

-Tighten the fist a fraction before you punch through the target.

-Drive in from your back leg.

Your left shoulder comes to meet your chin, which should be down as you are looking forward; my coach used to say "look through your eyebrows."

Do not drop your right or pull back like an archer when you throw your left.

In fact, there should be a slight movement across the face with the right hand (half an inch). Give your opponents nothing to hit, watch out for a hook as you move the right slightly in!

The jab hand must return to the defensive position immediately at eye level.

Never stay inside your opponent's effective range. Step back, or pivot to attack, or move away at an angle of 45 degrees (see Angles, Effective Range and Relative Safety).

Do not overreach. Work from effective range.

Tip: Bruce Lee said, "Be like water." I say, "Fighters need fluid movement."

Still More About Jabbing:

TIRED? HURT? NOT SURE WHAT TO DO? JAB. BUT NEVER THROW A SLOW JAB!

After Billy Duffin died, I did not box for quite a while, and I returned to another gym in Coventry.

Unusually, the gym I went to set up a ring to have me spar with a guy who had eight or nine consecutive knockouts. I was boxing at County level and they wanted to test him to see how far he could go. In the first seconds of the first round, the first punch he threw was a slow jab.

I rolled inside and hit him in the solar plexus. The guy was knocked out. Getting out of the ring took longer than the sparring. Never throw a slow jab.

Tip: During a fight, if you are tired, cut down on the number of punches, but maintain the quality. If you fail to do this, you will empower your opponent.

Aim to be the best in the gym at jabbing. It has many uses:

-Damaging

-Gauging distance

-Preventing an opponent attacking

-Buying time

-Setting up another punch e.g., straight right

-Blinding an opponent

-As a decoy

-As a power punch, used to break down opponents (see Golovkin vs. Lemieux).

-Scoring points

Ali used to corkscrew his jab to damage opponents, a technique invented many years earlier and reinvented by Ali.

De La Hoya dipped a little and punched up slightly, and opponents complained of whiplash.

We have a bag tethered top and bottom, and it's the jabbing bag. It's used for jabbing, and fighters repeat their jab, stepping in every time, normally 10 sets of 50 = 500.

Repetition makes the punch become a reflex action a perfect movement beyond thought.

Angles

When boxers refer to angles, they are referring to the angles of attack, exit, and their angle relative to the opponent whilst moving around the ring.

To take an opponent's right hand out of the equation, orthodox to orthodox, bring the lead leg to a position in line with the opponent's and their right hand will be removed from landing punches. You work your way to effective range and step in and over.

The normal attack, orthodox to orthodox, direct your lead leg directly into the opponent's groin. This sets up the straight right/overhand right perfectly.

Orthodox to orthodox, angle stepping away around 45 degrees to avoid left hook and right counters. Pivot and step away back foot first to get the head away with hands up and consider dropping level.

Telegraphing Punches

When your movements indicate your intentions, that is called telegraphing, and it can be catastrophically bad. You can be destroyed by an opponent if they can anticipate your attack.

Telegraphing and feinting cannot be confused: telegraphing warns of an impending move which is carried through, while feinting is a deception to garner a response. Telegraphing must be eliminated completely.

The most common telegraphing mistakes:

-Looking at the target area to be punched.

-Grimacing before the attack.

-Pulling hands back to enhance a blow.

-Lowering hands to punch.

-Clapping (yeah, really. I have seen this. It's not that uncommon).

-Punching in a regular and predictable way.

-Rotating hands to punch as they are over-rotated (turned inwards).

-Moving your head prior to attack.

-Adopting a defensive position with an arm prior to attack.

-Lifting the front foot or raising the toe part.

-Moving in without punching.

-Tipping head, shoulder, body.

-Shuffling *.

-Predictable rhythm or frequency.

*A tiny shuffle made before Jersey Joe Walcott threw his right in the 13th round in their 1952 bout telegraphed his intention and allowed Marciano, who was clearly losing, to land a right that resonated for decades.

https://www.youtube.com/watch?v=I9O3vxoOWbU

The First Punch

One of the major problems that beginners have in sparring, and especially in competition, is that the first punch often misses. That can be an issue of distance for sure, but also there can be some self-preservation going on, which can mean the fighter moves back faster than they move forward.

As soon as the fighter can, they should aim to throw several quality punches at a time while moving. This should occur in training, sparring and, of course, in competition, where it is essential.

Do not throw a solid punch, which often misses, followed by half punches. Those half punches are much more likely to land - a very common mistake. Make sure the following second and third punches are full punches with full force.

Have fighters training with guys they do not know; have a referee in the ring to get used to the distance and a third person in there before they compete.

Straight Right

The next punch to learn and perfect, a power punch unless used to set up an alternative punch, is the straight right. This punch may be used for head or body.

There is no exaggerated rotation of the back ankle in real boxing. It exists only in systemically flawed amateur "boxing" taught by amateur coaches all over the world.

It has gone on for years and truly cannot be found in professional fight films. with the exception of amateur-trained fighters who are disadvantaged automatically. There is no time for that twist, and it prevents movement. We never teach it and eradicate it if possible.

The straight right starts from the rear calf, and there is a minute movement as downward pressure is applied. The hip, torso, and shoulder rotate. In Cuba, some coaches tell the fighter to move their left shoulder back fast as the right moves forward, and, at the same time, to step in with their front foot, about one foot-length.

You may elect to simply sit down on the punch if your opponent is coming in hard or off the ropes. Then there is no need to step in unless you can time them and devastate with this punch.

Often the straight right is preceded by a straight left, and this creates the gap or forces the opponent to move, allowing the right to land.

Once the punch has landed, step back, pivot to attack, or move away at an angle of 45 degrees (explained later).

Point of interest: Old-time fighters hit the heart area with a power left or right to damage it during the fight. Bruising the heart would result in less blood and therefore less oxygen to the muscles.

Jack Dempsey advocated a paralyzing straight right to a southpaw's right bicep to eliminate the inconvenience of their jab by damaging the bicep. This is legal. You get no points for blows to the arms, but may obtain an advantage.

Tip: Have students cross their arms over their chest hands on shoulders.

-Rotate to the left as they step in front foot.

-Then, rotating to the right, bring the rear foot forward at the same time.

-Repeat this to fast-track coordination of movement.

-Legs don't move as fast as hands.

-If you move them first, you telegraph your intentions.

-If you move after, there is less mass.

-It has to be at the same time.

-Both feet on the ground when the blow lands.

-Glide feet just above the ground to keep contact. It's essential.

-Try punching with one foot off the ground. Told ya!

Overhand Right

This punch may finish a fight.

The overhand right is an extremely effective punch when landed. It involves a coordinated movement of the head to the left to avoid an opponent's jab whilst stepping in with a right that is slightly bent at the elbow. The punch hits the target (jaw) as it has access through the valley formed at the elbow as the opponent jabs.

It's probably better to use this punch later in a fight, especially if the opponent employs a lazy jab.

It is possible that the opponent will elect to throw a right, and that's not great as you are moving your head into the path of that punch. The reward may be worth the risk, however. You must practice this punch. It can be truly a devastating fight-ending blow.

I have bags set up in the gym with a rope in front with foam to enable the fighter to practice moving to the left of the simulated jab whilst moving in and landing the overhand right.

Tip: The key to being as efficient as possible in punching and movement is repetition.

There are exceptions to every rule, and Sergio Martinez had a spectacular overhand left used to KO Paul Williams. It was thrown with Martinez looking down with his head down and to the right. It was safe due to his head being low, and he committed to the punch and threw it several times until it connected in what was the KO of the year.

Tip: A basic feint to the opponent's body lays a trap; after jabbing heavily several times, throw an overhand right to the opponent's head.

Left Hook and Right Hook

A hook is devastating when landed correctly, especially if the opponent does not see the punch. The reality is that it takes time to practice and build up shoulder strength.

In order for a hook to be effective, you must rotate through the target with mass and acceleration, and the upper body rotates the arm and shoulder whipping round.

The hand position may be palm faced in or palm down. Either is legal.

Tip: We have our fighters do drills moving down a wall to prevent a wide arc telegraphing the punch.

The fighters also stand and, connected to bands with handles, throw technically perfect hooks stepping in.

Fighters that have a great left hook almost always punch with blistering speed - repetition.

Hooking requires shoulder strength, and we use weight and exercises to develop the deltoid muscles.

Note: The angle is always wider than you first imagine, and a lot of fighters never land hooks as:

1. They do not step in.

2. They throw at an angle that, at 45 degrees or more, cannot land. Some even arc in a way that could only ever be, at best, a glancing blow.

Never twist your front ankle. This is a monumentally flawed systemic amateur boxing issue. You simply never see professionals do this. Ask any trainer telling you to show you professional fighters doing this in real fights.

Don't take my word regarding twisting, just watch virtually every professional fighter on the planet, especially guys famous for hooking e.g., Jeff Lacy, Oscar De La Hoya, Micky Ward, Sam Langford, Sugar Ray Robinson, Danny Garcia and many others.

Interestingly, I read a book on Sam Langford that said that Sam used his right as often as possible to take attention away from his devastating left hook – possibly the best ever, and reserved for very dangerous opponents.

Keep your hooks tight, whip them in, through the target with full shoulder rotation. That's how to get real mass.

Always protect against a hook as the counter for a hook is a hook.

My favourite combination for southpaws: straight right, left hook.

I will deal with hooks to the body and solar plexus separately.

Rocky Marciano threw hooks to the opponents' arms in the absence of anything else. He hit so hard that opponents complained of bone fragments. One retired because his arm muscles were so badly damaged.

Close Quarter Power Hook

It is possible to summon the full body mass in a close quarter hook.

Step to the right back leg as you throw your hook, taking your whole body over to the right.

Your head and torso are safe from counter as they end up to the left of your opponent; this is a punch to use on the ropes.

This unusual punch can land very hard.

Check Hook

A hook incorporating a pivot, check hooks are normally used when the opponent is coming towards you attacking or coming off the ropes. Exquisite timing is required and therefore lots of practice and repetition as power is derived from the simultaneous pivot and hook.

I was trained to throw the check hook to avoid the opponent grabbing on to you as they fell; however, you also place yourself in complete safety at the side of your opponent as they move relative to your position.

We developed an attacking version of the check hook to obtain a superb attacking position with second hook from the side of the opponent.

Right Hook

Over the years, I would lean against opponents, my head on their shoulder, step back, and as they moved forward slightly, I would whip a right hook to the head.

Traditional right hook with the power hand does exist (see Tyson,

Holmes), but the opponent has to be in trouble or intimidated or both to enable a right hook from long range to land.

Frazier threw nothing but right hooks to head and body.

I once heard an MMA coach tell all students in a class that right hooks do not exist. Well, they do, but they are rarer than hen's teeth at long range, and as a selection I would go for the overhand right.

I work on a devastating pivot hook that works as the fighter disappears, hooking at the same time as they pivot to the right to end up at the side of the opponent.

Should you use right hooks?

Well, a lot may depend on your body type, boxing style and training.

If you throw a lot of hooks, they land, and you can slip/block/roll into range, why not?

If you are slower, the extra movement warns your opponent. At best, they can avoid or ride the blow. At worst, you get viciously countered.

Slipping or rolling orthodox inside to hook body: this is a counter rotational punch - hands high, step in, and roll under.

Pivot Right Hook

Pivoting through on the front foot to southpaw simultaneously whipping a right hook to the head, you are in effect shifting to full southpaw stance. Alternatively pivoting with a right hook feint then left hook from the side.

Hooks to Body and Head

The counter for a hook is a hook, so you have to be able to counter.

A hook to the head will bring a fighter's hand and arm up to protect as a reflex. That's your chance to double up and really sit down on the hook to the body (see Micky Ward). Hooking from body to head is easier. It flows better than hooking head to body. Either way, you really have to practice.

Tip: Landing punches to the body, using an in-and-up angle helps push air out the lungs, and, in the case of the solar plexus and liver shot, paralyzes the opponent.

Body blows can actually be more debilitating than head shots and certainly, down the road in longer fights, reap dividends as fighters slow.

Signs a fighter is hurt by a body blow:

-Fighters tend to drop their arms to avoid being touched again to the body.

-Fighters flatten their feet and may even move onto the ropes. You may hear air or sound from your opponent.

-If a fighter goes down, it could be a KO, as blows to the body can be brutal.

-There are two floating ribs, which you can crack reasonably easily.

Shovel hooks inside:

Left:
Power is derived from the front leg. The punch is angled up, palm turned in, and a short punch delivered with great force. As with uppercuts, the farther it travels, the lower the force imparted.

Right:
Same technique, but power is derived from the back leg.

Fighters can practice these punches at close quarters on bag, shield and body shield and develop astonishing power.

Both punches should be aimed at the torso and a slightly upward angled impact helps to debilitate the opponent, encouraging the air to be forced out of the lungs applying serious pressure to the rib cage and diaphragm.

Tip: Practice rolling in with hands up to maintain a tight defence and use the maximum body mass to create force with the hooks.

Tip: Old trainers tie the arms of fighters to their body to make them dedicate as much leg and body movement as possible. I use rubber straps at the elbows to hold the arms to their torso. The fighter wears a sweatshirt or long sleeved shirt to stop binding at the arms, and then the guys do this for weeks. Especially valuable to amateur fighters who may not have used their full punching potential ever.

Uppercuts

A short-range punch developed relatively recently in bare-knuckle days, the punch is vicious if it travels a short distance to find the target in a straight line.

Additional power can be incorporated by using the legs: left leg for left uppercut, right leg for right uppercut. Tie the arms to assist the fighter to find the maximum power.

Very effective against fighters moving in head down, the uppercut carries some risk as the head is momentarily exposed.

It is best practiced on a shield or mitts.

Tyson favourite: right hook to the body, right uppercut to the head.

Golovkin favourite: right uppercut to the head, left hook to the body.

Bolo Punch

This is named after the bolo machete used by Filipinos and combines a distraction with a swinging arm. Fighters have the option to use the arm that is swinging or the stationary arm, depending on which arm the opponent is not focussed on.

The bolo punch is rarely used, but effective, and visually spectacular. It requires practice in the mirror and is favoured by fighters such as Sugar Ray Leonard and Roy Jones.

The punch is a synergy of hook and uppercut. Using the static arm or using the fully rotating arm, the uppercut lands to body or head, depending on the position of the opponent, with the blow resulting at the end of full movement of the rotating arm.

Feinting

Of enormous value to a fighter, feinting is a skill we practice in the ring for many rounds. The fight team does 60 rounds a week.

If you are not punching, feint. If you are not feinting, punch.

Feint to prevent your opponent setting themselves.

Feint to break your opponent's rhythm.

Feint to stop an opponent's attack.

Feint to set up your own attack.

Feint to move your opponent into a position to be hit.

Feint to bridge a gap.

Feint on the pivot to hit or move away.

Feint to buy time.

Feint to move off the ropes.

It is a deception, the ability to totally deceive the opponent into believing a blow is definitely on the way so the opponent is forced to react to the perceived attack.

Many years ago, I was training in Tile Hill and a scruffy looking man came in wearing jeans, a dirty white t-shirt and old pumps - just a guy off the street.

Billy told me to spar with him and, frankly, he feinted me into oblivion. He was a superb fighter and it was actually a privilege to spar with him. He was far more experienced and skillful than I was - a superb boxer. I looked over at Billy, and he was chuckling away. James Cook was a really skilled fighter from that area who had fought at the highest level in the country.

The value of feinting is enormous, yet it uses so little energy.

Feinting causes stress and may destroy an opponent's rhythm.

There was a famous story about Willie Pep, so skilled that he feinted for an entire round, not throwing a single punch, and the judges awarded the round to him.

Feinting should be from the shoulders. It can be a subtle move of the body as long as you sell the idea that you are attacking. It takes time. It is a skill.

You had better learn it, or you will be at a severe disadvantage.

Feinting should always represent the exact initial movement of a real punch. It should be accompanied with leg movement to bridge the gap between fighters, to take advantage of the feint, and to land telling blows if your intention is to attack.

Feinting is wasted if you stop or move a fighter into a position to take advantage but fail to do so. The fighter feinting must move into position at the same time to land their punches; otherwise the opportunity is lost.

Feints take little energy and derive huge advantage. Fighters should refine this skill and work on it every day.

If you do not learn to feint, or if you underestimate its value, you are not fully equipped to fight. When faced with a close fight, lacking the skill of feinting can cost you dearly.

Warning: A feint is a deception. It is a slight body movement suggesting the danger of an imminent attack. To succeed, it must be totally believable and always only a slight movement, never extending the arm to render yourself vulnerable.

As you feint, it sets up the other arm to punch. Feinting then jabbing with the same arm works beautifully.

There is no skill that uses less energy in fighting and offers greater advantage. LEARN TO FEINT.

Traps: Employed in attack and defence, feints make an opponent unsure when your punches are genuine. They are the basis for traps that can fool even the greatest fighters.

Start off by punching hard to an area to establish that attack as a regular occurrence, then feint and attack should your opponent expose a target area whilst defending the feint. For example, feinting to the body overhand right to head.

The strange thing about the rhythm is that once a student starts to spar, we have to try to break the opponent's rhythm and take the opponent right out of their comfort zone.

My turn, your turn, my turn, your turn should not be the pattern when boxing. Ideally, it's never their turn.

The Ward vs. Gatti fights took a serious toll; don't try to emulate that. As glorious as wars are from a trainer's point of view, you don't want a fighter in that.

By feinting (the most underestimated of skills), moving, changing levels of punches, and varying combinations, angle and speed of attack, you should endeavor to dictate what is going; on in effect you are encrypting your boxing and the opponent cannot determine what is genuine.

Look at the masterful alternation of vicious attacks and counter punching of Marquez. His attacks alter Pacquiao's distance and make it easier for Marquez to time Pacquiao's attacks. Brilliant!

https://www.youtube.com/watch?v=NSn3wWoKz-k

Watch film of Willie Pep. one of the greatest and most skillful of all time:

https://www.youtube.com/watch?v=cLOlgphTN8c

Watch Sugar Ray Robinson:

https://www.youtube.com/watch?v=5VLWBVpL23k

Watch Sugar Ray Leonard:

https://www.youtube.com/watch?v=aX8YgLZvtUc

Watch Andre Ward:

https://www.youtube.com/watch?v=FAzb-vuG75A

Watch Juan Marquez:

https://www.youtube.com/watch?v=NpxiYu1rGsk

Watch Manny Paquiao:

https://www.youtube.com/watch?v=XK2nV0QaSbk

Distance

More fights are lost in the early stages of a fighter's career due to appreciating distance than any other factor.

Relative Safety

In boxing there is a position of relative safety which is a few inches beyond the opponent's reach after they have stepped in punching. This allows the fighter distance to defend. As the fighter gains experience, the distance of relative safety closes until you are only a little (fractions of an inch) outside the effective range.

Effective Range

The distance at which you can punch through the target is known as effective range; however, it is also your opponent's effective range.

As a fighter moves from relative safety to effective range, they must be moving in:

-Punching

-Parrying and punching

-Blocking and punching

-Rolling or slipping and punching

-Feinting

-Any of the above, but not walking in, as you will be hit.

Note: You must never attack from relative safety as you will land short and be seriously exposed.

Factors that determine relative safety are:

-The opponent's reach

-The opponent's speed - foot and hand

-The force the opponent hits with

-The kinds of punches the opponent throws.

Dealing with Distance

In the early stages of training and fighting, more fighters have problems with distance than anything else.

The biggest issue is that the distance for competition is greater than that for sparring, pad work and bag work. Consequently, fighters often attack from out of range, telegraphing their intentions and leaving themselves open to counter attack.

Getting close enough to land a blow with force is the issue: feinting, slipping, blocking, pivoting, counterpunching, rolling, even walking down the distance.

Most professional fighters are confident that they will land punches in a fight. The main question is: are they able to get their feet into a position to land punches with leverage and therefore force?

Bridging the gap to land punches with force is one of the fundamental skills of fighting. Once bridged, you are either landing a punch or moving your feet into position to do so. Once you have punched, you must either hit again or avoid being hit by moving away.

You are moving from "safety" to "effective range." The problem with being in effective range is that it is both yours and your opponent's.

Once you finish punching, you have got to get out of there. Pivot with hands high at 45 degrees away from the power hand, avoiding hooks, hands up, and perhaps dropping level.

Moving Off the Ropes

It can be as simple as an elliptical movement; kind of a large egg shape. You return to the middle of the ring; your opponent is now back to ropes. Move quickly into your opponent's left armpit, take shelter there and hold.

Check hook out of the corner/off ropes.

Take hold of your opponent, lean back and turn them onto the ropes, spinning them to their right fast. Utilizing your and their momentum, hit them as they will be off balance momentarily.

Treat the ropes like red hot elements. You hit them, you move.

Pivot hook out of the corner/off ropes.

Turn your opponent quickly, take their shoulders, lean back and spin them onto the ropes.

Move, ideally to your left, to obtain less resistance.

Cutting Down the Ring

Initial training must include understanding and dealing with the common mistake of following opponents around the ring.

If a fighter simply moves around the ring, the opponent has an unlimited distance to move backwards. The movement will severely reduce the effect of your punches; further, you burn up the same energy moving the same distance as your opponent unnecessarily.

Generally, moving to the right to cut down an opponent's movement is required.

Control of the Centre

To cut down the ring, take control of the centre.

This massively reduces the movement you make and places stress on your opponent as they are between the ropes and you.

Use angled movement, and feints to direct your opponent to the ropes or, even better, corner and attack. If you get too close in a split second, step back to gain extra mass, moving in again and hence, more force.

Wedge: Another option is to move at an angle squeezing your opponent into a corner as the pressure of your movement forces them into the position of being trapped in the corner.

Dealing with Speed and Counterpunchers

Now and again you will come across a fighter who is as fast or faster than you.

There are several options available:

1. Punch with them every time. They may have sacrificed mass for speed. If so, they will think twice before they attack if you punch harder.

2. Sway away from the first punch and catch them on the way in with your counter over the top.

3. Use feinting to destroy your opponent's rhythm.

4. Get medieval on the ropes and punch the speed out of your opponent.

Counterpunchers feed off of the initial attack.

Stand back and make them attack.

Work on angles and shifting to confuse them.

Double up on punches and encrypt your attack with feints.

Target Area

Amazingly, the target area is overlooked by trainers and fighters, who can go for years without a clear understanding. It is important to understand that the neck and throat are legal areas. The torso down to the navel is a point-scoring area.

Billy had me jabbing to the top of the head to follow up immediately with a right to the throat. He also favoured a hook to the carotid artery.

Like I said, he was the best.

The arms may be punched, but no points are accrued. In the absence of anything else, Marciano would hit the arms and shoulders to the extent that fighters would complain of bone fragments. One fighter had to retire, the muscles ripped off the bone.

Most effective legal areas to hit:

Head
Jaw
Neck
Throat
Biceps
Solar plexus
Ribs (especially floating)
Liver

Illegal Areas:

Blows to the back of the head, referred to as rabbit punches
Blow to the base of the skull, referred to as rabbit punches
Blows to the back of the neck, referred to as rabbit punches
Blows below the navel, referred to as low blows
Blows to any part of the back
Blows to the kidney area
Stamping on feet
Forearm blows to any area
Elbow blows to any area
Head to head
Head to body

Note: A referee may overlook blows if a fighter deliberately turns away from blows and invites blows to the back of the head in preference.

Dempsey punched opponents' biceps as hard as he could to paralyze their jabbing arms.

Fighters sometimes strike the opponent's arms, shoulders and hands to open up the defence to land telling blows. Conversely they may repeatedly strike an area to bring a fighter's arms down to prepare the ground for an alternative blow later. This is referred to as a TRAP.

It is accepted that amateur boxing is predominately about points, and amateur coaches are less concerned with leverage balance and realistic footwork.

Professional trainers are dedicated to getting the maximum leverage on punches. The trainer should always be mindful of a tight defence.

Leverage

To obtain maximum force punching:

Employ leverage (definition: The advantage gained by the use of a mechanism in transmitting force).

Employ flawless technique and timing.

-Develop strength and endurance in the muscles specifically involved in the punch or combination of punches.

-Break down the movement. Don't forget defence and the movement after the punch or combination.

-Study the exact foot position required to get maximum power from the legs relative to your opponent.

-Repeat the movement until it becomes a reflex action (beyond thought) moving in from your effective range, landing the blows and pivoting or moving away. You have to be able to relax.

Practice feints or combinations to achieve the position of leverage.

Each punch has leverage involved. A trainer must understand how to obtain the maximum force.

Employ a whipping action with hooks and pivot hooks. Check hooks. The breakdown should be the same.

Every punch must be through the target.

Timing takes time.

Understanding and anticipating your opponent's movement can gain advantage.

Combined with an appreciation of distance, timing is devastating if you can capitalize on your opponent's movement, often using their momentum against them.

This is an exquisite skill to possess and takes time.

Infighting

It does not follow that a long-armed fighter cannot fight inside.

The issue is can you get inside your opponent's guard? If you can, there is a wide selection of punches available.

If an opponent elects to hold, let them hold and keep punching. You get nothing for holding unless you are in trouble. It simply burns energy you could be using to punch, and the referee may permit the punching fighter to continue and not call break.

Moving forward as you infight can prevent the opponent being able to punch, as they are moving backwards and, best of all, gets your opponents off balance.

Infighting must be considered an essential skill, as the inability to do so means a fighter must rely on keeping the fight long range or tying up the opponent to prevent the use of this skill.

If a fighter succeeds in getting inside, then they must ensure the opponent pays dearly for the error in letting this occur.

Always protect your head. If you are looking for safety, force your head into your opponent's shoulder/armpit area.

Tip: Old-time fighters put a gloved left hand on the opponent's right bicep. The opponent cannot punch! Astonishingly effective, as there is no leverage to punch. Give it a try. You are able to throw your own right.

Controlling the Centre of the Ring

To conserve energy, a fighter should endeavor to impose their will and stake claim to the centre of the ring. Control of the centre enables a fighter to conserve energy which can then be used to punch more. Controlling the centre and cutting the ring down requires practice and discipline.

On a command to break, always turn your opponent and return to the centre. After you have attacked your opponent, return to the centre. The larger the ring, the less of an advantage you have, as you cannot impart stress as easily by pressuring your opponent on the ropes.

When fighters take control of the centre and use feinting to physically cut down the ring, they are applying constant pressure the way that Golovkin does. Fighters have commented that his punching force and unrelenting pressure break them down.

The objective of cutting the ring down is to trap opponents on the ropes and in the corners to deprive them of the ability to move away from blows and to be able to work from long range into short range with maximum leverage and then return to the centre.

Tip: As you cut down the ring, you will move from relative safety to effective range. You better be sure to be feinting, punching slipping or blocking, as you will be hit.

Warning: Walking into your effective range is dangerous because it is your opponent's as well.

Many combinations employed on the ropes are designed to punish fighters, moving from head to body and body to head. The more creative will be listed later.

Warm-up to Compete

I wrap the fighters' hands for amateur and professional fights early in the night. Then they can relax.

We take warm-up gloves, skipping rope, mitts, shield, body shield, and everything is set out. The fighter hands over their mouth guard and it is put in the fight bucket.

With around three fights (40 minutes) to go, we begin the warm-up.

Years ago, we would all stretch to prepare. However, fighters warm up beginning with very shallow light punches and movement. There is no stretching, just a gradual increase in length, movement and speed and working on combinations with confirmation on what to do.

Everybody has a plan until they get hit, so do not be so fixed on one strategy. Things change rapidly, sometimes to the fighter's advantage and sometimes not. Have an open mind and a Plan B.

I like my fighters really well warmed up. It reduces the chance of injury, and they can start fast, which is very important. Lots of excellent fighters have lost because they started off slow.

In a first round lasting 180 seconds, the warm-up had better have been done before they get in the ring. Let the opponent start off slow.

Some fighters are concerned that they do too much prior to getting into the ring. That's when they have to rely on the trainer's experience to get it right.

A calm professional approach is always best. See Roach, Sanchez, and Hunter.

Once the fighters are warmed, keep them warm; I cringe when there are huge ceremonial delays in the ring.

Tip: Remember, any nerves or concerns that you have are transmitted to your fighter. Keep them focused and take everything in your stride except any attempt by anyone to interfere with the warm-up process. Then you shield the fighter from this if possible and deal with it. I was at an MMA show and a fighter was shot after the show as he was rude to a fan prior to his fight. Try to keep the fighters focused mentally, warmed up, and sharp physically.

Working a Punch Bag

The quality of bags has never been better. There are some wonderful bags available, and they are relatively inexpensive.

Avoid rock-hard compacted bags - you will develop arthritis. Get rid of bags that compact or repack regularly.

The ideal heavy bag is one you can punch through the target 5" to 8".

I select bags very carefully. I use the best available, as they are hammered day and night.

I have springs attached to the bags. It helps give a little, and we try to ensure the bags can all be adjusted for opponents' heights by adding chain at the top.

Some bags are marked or numbered for punches. We often tape the bags for level.

For hockey players, we add material around the bag to hold to simulate holding and hitting.

Training is different for lacrosse players: I use 1-minute, 2-minute, 3-minute periods with 15-to-30 second rests.

I train the fighters super hard on the bags as there is no wear and tear in the sense that the fighters are not knocking lumps off each other.

Movement on the Bag

Circling round a bag flicking punches takes some effort, but you are not really punching through the target, and that is manifestly flawed. Fighters develop this movement because the bags, old and compacted, are too dense to hit, so they develop a style of boxing which has more to do with avoiding damage to their hands because of the condition of the bags they hit. That is unbelievable.

A realistic approach means you must step towards your opponent (bag) and pivot away to avoid being hit. Watch professional fighters, look at their movement, and note how they step in to punch. Do not move how you think fighters move, but move as they actually do. Keep it real, especially on the punch bag. Punch from your defensive hand position on the way in and never drop your hands on the way out.

Sometimes we use a rail or rope to keep the feet and fighter correctly positioned whilst hitting a bag. Sometimes the rope would be positioned to step over. When we train the fighters to simulate the position of fighters, left leg in line with their opponent's to take their right hand out of the equation completely and have fighters step forward and to the left at the same time to attack, then step away at an angle.

Tip: Never walk in to hit a bag. You must punch, slip, block or feint your way in. Never drop your hands on the way out.

Your hands should return at the same speed as they punched out.

Fighters often drop their arms whilst bending whilst working; it is a crazy move. Keep your arms up! Whilst the fighter may feel it looks stylish, it's actually suicidal.

One of the greatest training techniques we use, which I invented, is sharing an anchored bag, with one fighter on one side and one on the other.

1st minute: left hand jabs, hooks, uppercuts, stepping in and back, pivoting.

2nd minute: right hand straight right, hooks, uppercuts, stepping in and back, pivoting.

3rd minute: Both hands fast 10s left, right, hooks, uppercuts - unleash hell.

It forces fighters to be able to punch independently with each arm by being able to get the muscle groups work easily moving from punch to punch in a way that is technically correct with terrific intensity and no wear and tear on the fighters - just the hardest training possible. This makes the training at Sugarrays much tougher than other clubs as the bags are there to be hit 100 percent of the time.

Further, with the bag tethered top and bottom, there is simply no rest period. Fighters punch more, so the they get more from every training session. Finally, you must make sure fighters step in and pivot away to keep it real.

Drills for Bags

Left (jab): start off jabbing; I either tether a bag or instruct the fighter to step in with the front foot, hit the bag and step back. As the bag returns, the fighter must hit it again and so on. Repeat 50 times 10. Be careful not to hyperextend arm; punch from defensive position; make sure the shoulder comes to the chin; hit high on the bag; don't forget a slight move across the face. Right hand force is derived from the back leg, stepping in and rotation of the torso, and acceleration of the arm.

Left right: stepping in (front foot), throw a left right step back and repeat.

Left shoulder comes to chin throwing the left right shoulder as you throw the right.

Punch from the defensive position.

Do not pull hands back, drop hands, make faces, or telegraph in any way.

Punch as you step, but your foot is on the ground as you land.

Left or right hook: before one works on combinations, perfecting your hook and ensuring you are throwing it with enough force requires some time. Correct technique takes practice. Stand beside a wall and step forward, throwing your hook over and over. The wall prevents swinging wide and makes the punch difficult at first, but later very fast. Normally thrown in combination with other punches, the transfer elbow high shoulder protecting the chin a wider angle for your arm than 45 degrees ensures contact as it enables your hook to pass around. The lead arm must ideally be whipped right through the target. Stand to the side of the bag and step in throwing a hook, stepping in as you punch. Repeat over and over.

Defence

Hone your defence as soon as you can. You cannot be too careful and, all things being equal, the tighter your defence, the more likely you are to win. But remember, you must land your punches to be judged effective.

My final pre-fight instruction: "do your job – land your punches."

Success and failure can be measured in fractions of a second. Keeping your chin down and your hands up is a great start.

I favour a traditional hand position but concede that it can depend on the fighter. Arm length, height, weight, and speed can all come into play.

One extreme example of tailored styles is Mike Tyson, who used constant lateral movement to get close enough to land heavily, making his opponents question the safety of trying to land punches. This style exactly complemented his height, weight and explosive punching when in position.

Marciano fighting from a crouch was deceptively hard to hit. Ali had serious trouble hitting him when they sparred for their film long after Rocky retired.

Joe Frazier's all-action, forward pressure bending hooking style gave Ali serious problems. The list goes on....

Philly defence is flawed. An opponent's arcing overhand right finds a home whilst forcing the defender to concentrate on not getting hit, and often the defensive fighter is unable to counter as he places too much weight on the back foot to hit effectively from that stance. They are looking for an uppercut counter or straight right using power from the back leg, and thus, there are inherent problems if the defensive fighter's balance/counter is affected by the aggressive attack.

See Broner vs. Maidana.

https://www.youtube.com/watch?v=eU-8mLEp5sA

The jab from the waist favored at the Kronk Gym for many years conserved energy, but an opportunity for a right counter from very fast hands exists, so I believe it has serious issues.

I like a defence that automatically gives a fighter a counterattack. I also like a defence that keeps a fighter right in the fight all the time, as you only win by landing punches.

Don't get me wrong. There is nothing wrong with fighters touching opponents and setting up combinations by putting the opponents where they want them. Nor is there anything wrong with taking a walk and frustrating a fighter with movement. It's just that at the end of the day, a tight defence balance technique pays dividends. Hamed vs. Barrera would be an example.

You get no points for defence in boxing, it has always been that way. People pay to watch amateur and professional boxing and expect to see a competitive fight; therefore, fights are always judged on effective aggression. Without a tight defence in boxing, however, you are unlikely to win and you may end up seriously hurt.

Before any fighters spar they must practice their movement and do drills in the ring. The first drills involve movement whilst coordinating punching with defence.

"The only time you can be hit is when you drop one or both hands." - Gene Tunney

I have the fighters' hands at eyebrow height when in effective range. In relative safety, they can relax the position, and, if you observe professional fighters, they often raise their guard as they move forward.

Block and Blocking Incorporating Elbows

This is a physical obstruction using the arms. Since you get no points for blows to the arms, it is extremely effective.

Tip: when blocking to the body, bend knees and prepare to punch immediately with the arm not blocking, using the force generated by legs, torso and counter-rotation. Practice this so it is a reflex action.

Blocking hooks to the head, throw a counter hook immediately as you block. The primary reason for this is that fighters often drop the right whilst hooking with the left.

Don't be feinted into dropping your arms then hit to the head. Always bend at the knees.

A legal and super-efficient way to block is to bring your elbow into play to collide with the bicep of the opponent. I have seen the bicep ripped by such a simple adjustment of the angle of the elbow. The thing is, the harder the opponent hooks, the worse it is for them, with little to no effort from the defending fighter. The timing for this is exquisite; however, it does open the possibility of a body blow. The risk may be worth the reward. At the very least, the opponent will think twice about hooking and may not understand what actually happened.

When blocking hooks to the body, it's possible to use elbows by stabbing down an inch or so as you bend your knees slightly. This will damage the hands and especially the thumbs of your opponent as they try to hook your body if the elbow collides.

Parry

The term come from the French "to ward off."

A parry may involve a redirection of a blow with an open hand, often the defensive dominant hand.

The key to parrying is to hit, at the same time stepping in.

You are redirecting the blow to use your opponent's mass as they move forward combined with your blow.

Common mistake: to parry then counter. The opportunity to land a punch fails as that is too slow. The parry and counterpunch must be almost simultaneous.

Common mistake: moving your hand forward rather than tapping the opponent's punch over your shoulder. The parry is like a very fast wiper blade that always returns to defensive position.

Common mistake: freezing the hand at the right side of your head, leaving you horribly exposed.

Common mistake: to parry and step away all the time. You are not getting hit, you are surviving, but you are not winning either.

Slap parry: a version done with either hand, meeting the opponent's punch to neutralize it early

Drills to parry: initially moving in the ring, taking turns to parry several times.

Make sure the fighter does not step away.

Make sure the hand does not move to meet the opponent's punch.

Later advanced – three-minute rounds in the ring. To keep it real, fighters take turns parrying, but I introduced a rule that if a fighter lands his jab, he automatically gets another turn. They may feint to body or head.

Slip

A slip is movement inside or outside a punch, using your nearest arm to further shield your movement in a blocking fashion. For a slip to be effective and enable you to land a blow, you must step in. Your feet need to be in the correct position in relation to your opponent to land a blow with leverage. I sometimes describe this as rolling inside and outside.

The advantage of slipping outside punches is that you are unlikely to get hit. This can involve the right foot shifting forward, and then you have leverage to punch to the ribs.

The advantage of slipping inside is that you have a wonderful opportunity to hit to the solar plexus and the area is very exposed. There is, however, a danger that you could be countered with a right.

To practice this, do drills in the ring with your trainer watching.

Practice on the bag moving in against an imaginary opponent's jab.

Sway

Sway is very effective when used to take the venom out of a fast puncher's attack as you take your centre of gravity with you so you can come over the attack of your opponent with your counter attack. Moving away like that makes the opponent doubt their ability to hit you, and they can lose confidence in their initial attack.

It is essential to take your bottom fist back as you need to retain that stability and the ability to respond with punches.

To sway, straighten front leg as you step back slightly with your back leg, say 4", to avoid the initial attack. As you take your bottom with you, the centre of gravity is preserved; thus you can hit with full force.

You could consider:

-Straight right left hook
-Double jab
-Left right

As counters:
-Riding punches
-Styles of defence
-Defence on the ropes
-Moving off the ropes

Speedballs

Not all amateur and professional clubs have speedballs, even if they have the frames. The best trainer I ever had did not have a speedball or frame in the gym.

So often, you see guys working out on the bags and skipping doing their exercises. Then they realize the limited effort it takes to get skillful on a speedball, and they focus on the speedball. Trainers then watch potential fighters going down a path of less resistance.

Fighters at the Kronk Gym in Detroit would trap the speedball using their up jab. Joe Frazier would adjust to his opponent's height to hook. I would use it only as a warm-up/cool-down exercise and did not use one. As I said, we did not have them.

Speedballs are useful for warming up, and the noise is paradoxically both intrusive yet welcoming as one enters a gym. The rhythmical noise belongs in the gym, so, despite my experience, I always provide a speedball, since they are synonymous with the sport.

A few years ago, I commissioned an artist to work with stainless steel to make a sign depicting a speedball for the exterior of the gym. Instead, he kept the dimensions and drawings I had given him, creating a piece of art for himself.

Digging Deep

Fighters need to dig deep into themselves to win. So many people ask to be pushed, and the problem with this is that boxing is so much about digging deep into your reserves of fitness and pushing yourself. Strength and sheer will power are required, and you have to be able to access these during a fight. You have to dig deep.

Marquez throws rocks in the mountains of Mexico to develop the exact muscles to enhance punching power.

Minter ran with house bricks.

Ali ran in army boots.

Frazier hit sides of meat (an idea inspired by Joe and used in the Rocky film).

Fitzsimmons used an ironmonger's forge.

We use ropes for climbing to strengthen hands, wrists, shoulders and backs. The ropes provide awesome functional training. Chris Eubank climbed a rope to gauge his strength and endurance and to determine how close he was to being ready approaching a fight. Back in the day it was an Olympic discipline, and men could climb 20 feet in 3 seconds, arms only. That's astonishing!

Battle ropes can cause rotator damage, so we tend to avoid those. Further, the margin for error using heavy weights is way too slim to incorporate it for fighters making a living at regular jobs. It is too dangerous to do as a training for fighters, as they need to be 100 percent on the day.

We will look at rope pulling and dragging through bars to obtain resistance. We favour body weight exercises for strength and endurance at Sugarrays. We do not have conditioning coaches, preferring to do everything in-house the old way. A lot of trainers are returning to this now.

Underqualified, inexperienced cross training classes are the latest craze. Pushing reps and weights higher can only result in failure- sometimes catastrophic. Boxing is cheaper, and you develop a defensive skill. Further, one could argue that every aspect of the training of the fighter has stood the test of time.

A huge advantage, speaking as a trainer of fighters, is that by doing the conditioning in-house you are not subject to the treacherous behaviour of people you deigned to give a chance. How quickly they forget! Look what happened to Freddie Roach, one of the all-time greats when he placed trust in a "conditioning coach".

Using a Timer

We are designing an app right now to enable students and gyms to use our timing system easily for circuits, ring work and bag work. We find the cheapest way is to use a TV, so we mount flat screens and they are awesome. You can use Comcast to support the TV, and it can all be connected remotely.

The app will offer superb bag training with the option of coaching, especially prompts for speed, hand position, stepping back and stepping in, and fast 10 second bursts.

Training on Mitts

As a trainer, you must know how to work with mitts or your fighter will be less effective and you will eventually damage your arms at the elbow joints.

There are many men who are charging for training and training on the Internet who are incompetent.

Your hands should be inside your shoulders and the mitts at the opponent's head height or the fighter's if they don't have an opponent.

Keeping hands inside the shoulders:
1. Takes strain off your elbows.
2. Keeps it real for the fighter with tighter punches to the head area.

Any trainer holding the mitts for beginners that cannot move properly are doing them no favours. They must be able to move properly and coordinate hands and feet.

You should take punches moving the mitts towards your own face to keep the whole thing real (watch Freddie Roach), but do not let fighters hit you on the jaw.

Try to move back as opponents do. This will force your fighter to move and hit.

Work slowly, methodically, and speed up gradually as you strive for perfection.

Do this on all combinations.

Do not be fooled by Mayweather's choreographed garbage. That's for public consumption and bears no resemblance to what's required to fight. I saw a fighter warm up with his uncle using that choreographed method, and he lost every round in a professional fight.

Do not slap at punches thrown. You see this a lot. It's bad for the fighter, can damage the fighter's wrists, and is frankly incorrect.

Keep it real. Make the fighter move.

Move towards your fighter fast to simulate attacks also.

As the trainer, your responsibility is to ensure that fighters' balance, movement, punching and defence are as good as they can be.

The punches have to be viable; that is, there MUST be full leverage and defence and everything has to be tight in order to ensure maximum speed.

Tip: there are two kinds of speed to work on the mitts.

Speed of Movement

The feet do not move as far as the arms (except when shifting).

The faster they move, the more effective the fighter is likely to be, but everything must be coordinated.

Speed of Combinations

Punches should be coordinated. They should flow and should be blisteringly fast through the target.

If you are not sure how fast, say BANG BANG BANG fast, and that's how quickly they should land with full force in the gym with 16-ounce gloves.

Fighters move in punching. You should have both feet on the ground on hitting the target. Punch through the target.

As a trainer, I advise you to buy the best mitts shield and body shield available. The very best are currently Winning, made in Japan.

When calling combinations to the fighter, keep it real. Look at what fighters actually throw in fights. I advise trainers not to make up combinations. That takes experience.

We use three punch combinations and add feints, pivots and shifting in the middle of the ring and on the ropes.

Keep It Real

Standing still with a fighter hitting the mitts is boxercise.

Failing to check the movement, defence and force purely sucks.

If a fighter is inaccurate, they can damage your hands. Put them back on a bag and tape targets.

Don't massage the ego of fighters, or your own, by trying to fast track. I have seen so many coaches create problems for others by doing this. It's selfish and unprofessional.

Training on Shields (Held)

Massively underrated and one of my favourite pieces of equipment.

I work extensively with shields and love them. The Title $40 shield is as good as they get. We have almost 20 of them.

Shields are great for combinations of hooks and uppercuts, shovel and solar plexus work.

Training on Body Shields

Absolutely essential if you are a serious coach.

We use Winning mitts and body shields.

Using them increases the speed you can demand from your fighter head-to-body, body-to-head.

So much more efficient. The trainer can get far more work from a fighter than with mitts alone.

Shadowboxing

Never underestimate the value of shadowboxing.

Do three-minute rounds

After skipping/roadwork, Sugarrays fighters do nine rounds every day:

-3 Shadow all full movement punching and stepping in/ pivoting movement.
-3 Feinting full movement.
-3 Pivoting moving in and away.
-3 Shifting forward with feints.

I watch the fighters' every move every day.

I watch 60 rounds of shadowboxing every week.

Pacing

Many fighters lose as they burn out punching too much, too quickly and exhaust themselves before the fight is completed. It's a common issue.

The objective is effective aggression – TO WIN.

You can take your opponent into deep water, but you cannot be the one to drown.

Do not throw all your punches in the first 30 seconds. Be clinical, apply pressure by feinting, by moving, and by landing punches, either by attacking or counter-attacking. Controlling the ring, controlling the fight, fighting your fight at your pace even if you have had to adjust to an opponent's style.

Do not be lulled into an easy fight pace that suits your opponent. That was Hopkins' style, banking rounds by slowing the pace. If you think about it, he did worse against opponents who fought their fight at their pace, taking him out of his comfort zone.

Make your opponent more concerned about what you are doing than what they should do.

Don't ever go back to the corner saying, "I would have won if it had gone a few more rounds."

As a trainer, I cannot ask for more than 100 percent from a fighter. As a fighter, you have to be able to dig deep, fight your fight, impose your will, and effectively land your punches.

Do not squander energy; be accurate. Wyatt Earp's "fast is fine, but accuracy is everything" applies to boxing just as it does to gun fighting.

As a fighter, you may have to give more than 100 percent.

Time flies. Shine brightly and enjoy your moment under the bright lights. What you do will last a lifetime. What you achieve is directly proportional to the effort you invest and that is true of everything in life.

Pace yourself but make it as effective as possible - impose your will.

Never come back and say you could have done more.

Adapt during the fight and find a way to win.

Safety Precautions

Head guards do not prevent damage to your brain, but they do prevent cuts from clashes of heads. Some fighters prefer not to wear one. which is absolutely crazy. It's unprofessional, and you can be injured to an extent that your career as a fighter is ended by a serious cut that can reopen in future fights.

I fired a trainer who would not wear one to spar.

The only cuts I sustained (two) were in fights due to clashes of heads.

This does not even touch on the issue of cross contamination by blood, which could be life changing and possibly life threatening.

Buy a quality head guard. Rival is great and, of course, Winning is currently the very best - but expensive.

A head guard with bar helps prevent damage to your nose and lips. We recommend these, but only quality makes. You don't want something as bulky as a motorbike helmet.

Mouth guards are worn to protect your teeth, and damage from teeth. Get the best possible.

Dentist-made are wonderful, home-moulded are pretty good, and, if they fit well, they're great.

I used to recommend a slight pinch at the sides to ensure it holds in place as it's cooled in the home-moulded type.

Tip: wear your mouth guard and head guard whilst hitting the mitts and bags to get used to them.

It's hot and uncomfortable. Welcome to the toughest sport on the planet.

Sparring must be controlled. This is where you learn to fight, and you must ensure that fighters respect the ring, the gym and the safety protocols.

All instructions must come from the trainer.

Tip: put a referee into the ring as well, so novices are used to a third man prior to competing.

I like controlled punching, especially to the head, say 50 percent power to head and 60 percent to body. Some of our fighters wear thin body shields so fighters can go at 100 percent to the body.

As a trainer, stop heavy hooks and severe straight punches to the head immediately.

Tip: as a fighter, match force with force and never continue to take punches waiting for a trainer to intervene. Don't get me wrong. I am not advocating a war, but it's absolutely essential that you do not take heavy blows while you wait for a trainer. You could be badly hurt.

Be wary of fighters who want to keep it light and then look for an opportunity to hit hard once they have the confidence to do so.

I saw one former world title holder insisting a fighter be lighter in sparring with him, then he tried to hurt that fighter with the best punches he could throw. It was a pretty disgusting thing to see.

As a trainer, you are totally in control. Look for any learning points, and stop the sparring if profound mistakes are being made at any level.

We film sparring and I use a 10' Tripod so the filming takes in footwork as well as the action. If a fighter is knocked down, send the opponent to a neutral corner, and begin a count. The fighter has to be on his feet by "eight." If not, stop the sparring.

If the fighter gets up, caution the opponent to take it easy and resume boxing.

Invite other clubs to bring fighters. It's great to get used to the added distance and different styles of fighters.

Sometimes an opponent is more style than substance. Make sure you land your punches.

Training

Gym Warm-up:
-Skipping/ Cycle/ Rowing/ Running
-Up to 30 minutes 30 seconds push-ups for skipping with no rests
-Reps of 10 abdominal exercises increasing to 50 of each kind
-Push-ups 10-9-8-7-6-5-4-3-2-1 or 1-2-3-rest,1-2-3 rest to exhaustion
-Chain Training, working up to 4 x 50
-Rope Climbing
-Weights
-Bag work 3/5/8/10 rounds against an opponent other side of bag - utterly exhausting.
-Technical training on the mitts
-Sparring in the ring (filmed)

So we start with 3 sessions a week:
Mon. Wed. Fri.
Progress to 4 days a week:
Mon. Wed. Fri. Sat.
Competitive 5 days a week:
Mon. Tues. rest Thu. Fri. Sat. rest (days just for example).

Sessions for fighters may be two a day and involve conditioning, sparring, technical circuits.

For circuits, we favor a Tabata clock with interval building to 50 seconds on and 10 seconds to move.

We have a cardio section and a weights section and a rope climbing element. The circuit operates for hours and is brutal, but it has the advantage that you work at your level.

Road work for boxing would be an hour of running no more than three times per week, with as many hills as possible to replicate the herculean effort involved in boxing, with rest in between. Explosive sprinting towards fights is important.

In general, the training works on 3-minute rounds, but to be sure fighters get off fast in 2-minute fights, we have to do 2 minutes training closer to amateur fights.

The fight team train additionally every morning Monday to Friday.

The best exercise for punching is punching. The best way to do this to build strength and cardio by building up muscles with weights and functional training then rounds on a punch bag and mitts honing technique and endurance.

The muscles for boxing are easily identified but broadly:

Calves
Quads
Hamstrings
Glutes
Lower back
Abdominal
Intercostal
Obliques
Chest
Triceps
Deltoid
Biceps
Neck and Jaw – to absorb the odd blow
In addition, you require great hand strength and forearm strength.

A fighter's requirements suggest that heavy weights are less important than sustained explosive endurance, so we go for lighter weights and work to the limit.

Our chains get progressively heavier when lifted and encourage an explosive movement.

The use of lighter weights encourages endurance and speed and removes the possibility of serious injury, common with heavy weight lifters.

Keep away from cross-training clubs. The instructors lack experience and have a track record of producing injury. The idea is to push the members to increase reps and weight. This can only end in failure and with heavy weights, the real possibility of injury exists

Corner Work

One person is permitted in the ring, normally the chief second.

If the fighter is cut, the chief second may elect to have a cut man in the ring while the chief second works from outside the ropes.

You have 60 seconds, with a 10-second warning to conclude work.

Round ends by bell, then this sequence:

-Stool in first.
-Chief second or cut man in.
-Sit fighter down make sure legs are straight.
-Remove mouth guard and place in icy water.
-Place ice bag on neck.
-Tell fighter to close eyes.
-Spray face with icy cold water.
-Towel face, but the fighter must not blow nose (may cause eyes to swell).
-Possible Vaseline application to eye brow, orbit and cheek area. I use frozen as it is thicker.
-Swab up nose with adrenalin.
-Sip of water. May spit or not.
-Instructions should be clear and simple.

-Ask the fighter what you said to confirm.
-Sip of water.
-Insert gum shield.
-Remove ice pack.
-Stand fighter up.
-Stool out.
-Final confirmation of instructions at rope side.

Calm is best. Some fighters need to know if they lost a round, but it's more important to tell them how to win the next. Honesty between fighter and trainer endorses the trust.

The referee or doctor may visit the corner. A boxing commissioner may be positioned to ensure fair conduct.

Cut Man Kit

I carry:
Avitene
Adrenaline (Epinephrine) 1/1000
Endswell
Ice Pack Ziploc bags, large (cheap)
Cotton wool
Cotton buds
Butterfly stitches
Glue
Scissors Surgical
Gloves
Tape
Avitene Powder for coagulation (legal), Dry cut – apply powder- apply Vaseline.
Adrenalin 1/1000 liquid for constricting capillaries. Dry cut, place swab or soaked adrenalin (Epinephrine) or Q-tip onto cut and hold as long as possible. Apply Vaseline. This causes the capillaries to constrict, stopping bleeding.
Frozen Vaseline over cut. Frozen is better as you can apply more.

Q-tip inside nose with Avitine mixed with Vaseline or adrenalin-soaked Q-tip

For nosebleeds, tip head forward.

Never get the person to blow their nose as eyes may swell.

I carry a commercial enswell that is icy cold and should have Vaseline on it to avoid injury to the fighter.

I prefer a stainless Ikea tin with lid that I fill with a little ice and then tape shut. I have had it for years.

Do not push swellings across face unless dire. Apply the enswell to the swelling and let the ice cold do its job.

Numbering Punches

I tend to call the punches by name for beginners, but work by numbers with advanced fighters, if they prefer.

Since we work in three-punch combinations to guarantee force, numbers are less important. Don't trot out numbers that force fighters to make ineffective combinations.

1 jab
2 cross
3 left hook
4 right hook/overhand right
5 left hook body
6 right hook body
7 left uppercut
8 right uppercut
9 left shovel hook
10 right shovel hook

Cus D'amato's numbering:

1 left hook jaw
2 right hook jaw
3 left uppercut
4 right uppercut
5 left hook body
6 right hook body
7 jab head
8 jab body

D'Amato used a numbered target made of mattresses to train his fighters.

Bags are available now already-numbered, or you could number them.

Cheating

Not because you should, but because you should know what goes on.

Influence of PPV:

Some appalling decisions over the years have resulted to preserve a title or move a "winning" fighter towards a future super event. There have even been decisions that point to home country advantage.

Something must be done to control all the boxing organizations, addressing what's good for boxing, for the fans, and for fighters as well as what is equitable to boxing organizations.

Promoters

Promoters twist and turn to obtain advantage, and they should be watched carefully.

There are new promoters emerging and some that operate with a low profile rarely seen and have done so for years. It takes all kinds, and there is always going to be corruption and influence when huge amounts of money are at stake. If there is the power and opportunity to do something good, then the reverse may also apply.

The public are not stupid and will lose interest. Why would people pay to watch fights where fighters have records that suggest they cannot possibly win and do not justify the opportunity to fight? Guillermo Rigondeaux, a very skillful boxer with the punching power of a newborn kitten, was fed-glass jawed fighters to stimulate public interest, but he could not knock them out them. It doesn't work if you haven't got it.

I have met boxers who have gone to Cuba and come back worse than when they went. That is no surprise in a country committed purely to amateur boxing.

Protect by Research

Do research to protect your fighter. Take the full name of the opponent make sure the spelling is correct and Google 30 pages back to ensure the experience is correct. Check YouTube and Facebook.

Go to the weigh-in and, if the opponent weighed in early, have them reweigh.

Attend draws. Go to the draw for fighters in tournaments. Go to pre-fight briefings.

Wraps and Gloves

Always inspect the other fighter's hand wraps and gloves for weight. Make sure the opponents only use surgical tape and that hands are legally wrapped. Some fighters make their hands into clubs by overwrapping in tape, simply winding over and over. Layering is the practice of putting tape between the layers of bandage: tape/bandage /tape/bandage. It is illegal. Starching/adding plaster to wraps to make them hard is also illegal. Unhappy? Get them changed.

I have seen fighters hit a wall to break down the padding in their boxing gloves prior to fighting. Are the gloves even the correct weight? The manufacturers tab is often wrong. Examine all the fight gloves available and select if possible.

Rules and Scores

In tough man contests, the rules are sketchy. Dodgy result? Check scorecards. If a score is very close, check the judges' scorecards. It's not hard, and you have the right. There are only three judges.

Low Blows

If a fighter is far ahead, too strong or too fast, the opponent may deliberately hit low. The offender often does this with the side shielded from the referee unless he wants to be disqualified.

The referee may not acknowledge a series of low blows. I had one fighter who was hit low four times with no opponent deductions, suggesting a home town advantage. At that stage, I feel it is appropriate to fight fire with fire, and I would instruct my fighter to reciprocate.

If you get hit low and the ref does not see it, the judges must ignore the infringement.

Quite often, an offending fighter may also punch the thigh of the opponent to slow him down.

Slapping

Hitting with the inside of the glove is illegal. Fighters do this to increase their reach and alter distance. Some referees do not consider it a point-losing issue.

Illegal is illegal and that is how it should be viewed.

Spitting out Mouth Guards

Fighters sometimes spit out mouth guards to buy time. The pressure on the referee to have it washed and returned to the opponent is huge. Years ago, I saw a fighter seriously bite his tongue, and it was an awful injury. A bucket was brought to the fighter, and he was in a bad way.

The referee should:
-First time, warn.
-Second time, deduct a point.
-Third time, disqualify.

Spitting out the mouth guard is a dangerous illegal practice.

Head-butting

Accidental clashes of heads are often predetermined. Whilst these collisions may not be totally intentional, a fighter will sometimes lower his head, coming lower in and up into the brow or face of the opponent colliding with his forehead. This can be cynical, deliberate and career-ending. You have to be very careful to protect your head.

There are fighters out there who, while not deliberately butting, have a technique that ensures that when a clash of heads occurs, they will come off better.

It's like an insurance policy, so you have to watch these guys. If you are head-butted, you have to take the blame as it's up to you to protect yourself. I had a few nasty clashes and a couple of blatant butts and felt I should have been warier. One fighter came off the ropes and crushed the cartilage in my nose, totally deliberately. I should have been more careful.

I was boxing for the County and a guy from Liverpool spun round as I moved in, hooking off my jab. The back of his head hit my eyebrow and I sustained a hideous cut. He should have been disqualified immediately, but I don't know what happened because I had to go directly to hospital for sutures. I take full blame for being butted, but I had never seen anything like it before or since.

The reality is that because some fighters move forward, dipping and coming up at the point of contact, their forehead will always hit your face. This is no accident. It is an elliptical move to ensure any damage is always sustained by you.

Sometimes you can get caught by a fighter coming off the ropes head first. Southpaw and orthodox are notoriously prone to collision. You have to protect your head, as damage can quickly change the nature of a fight and the result.

In a 1980 Glasgow bout, Shaun O'Grady sustained a head-butt fighting Jim Watt. O'Grady appealed to the ref, and Watt hit him hard as he did so. It was a fight-changing event and rescued Watt's title.

O'Grady made two errors:
1. To get butted.
2. To take his eyes off Watt to protest.

Never take your eyes off your opponent.

https://www.youtube.com/watch?v=uFZHzNw3IKQ

I have a friend, who, in his first fight as a professional, sustained a butt in the final seconds of the last round. It was a deliberate and vindictive act by a fighter who lost every round, but the fault for the butt being landed rests with the recipient. You must protect yourself at all times.

Illegal and Questionable Practices

Abrasion:
Abrasion can occur during the fight if the opponent rubs his rough beard on the brow, thinning the opponent's skin around the eye like sandpaper.

Kneeing on the Ropes:
Kneeing occurs as a fighter's back hits the ropes. They lean back and raise the front leg, and it contacts the opponent's groin.

Cuffing and Thumbing:
Cuffing is the practice of pushing the palm and cuff up the face of the opponent, damaging the face and taking balance. Thumbing is obviously an attempt to blind an opponent. Sam Langford finally retired during a fight when a fighter thumbed him in the eye. He had partial vision due to cataracts (the optic nerve having been severed in the other eye in a previous fight). He became completely blind - very sad end for perhaps the greatest fighter of all time.

Knee Knock:
This is subtle and totally illegal move. The fighter places his front leg inside the opponent's when the opponent is on the ropes. The rotation as you wind up to hook rotates the body to the right, and your leg deliberately destabilizes the opponent's leg. This drops the opponent's level and often their left arm, opening an opportunity for a hook.

Arm Lock:
In the early days, boxing also included wrestling, but now the wrestling has for the most part been phased out. If a fighter elects to wrestle with you, allow them to do so and keep punching.

Judges ignore the wrestling, and a ref may let you continue to punch until he decides to call break. This is a point-scoring opportunity.

Arm locks, whist illegal, tie up an arm and may distract the fighter who is locked, and you could capitalize with telling shovel hooks or uppercuts.

Astonishingly, simply placing your hand on your opponent's bicep, left hand inside and onto the right bicep, stops any attempt to throw the punch.

Arm Breaking:
I have seen this live and once over the years on TV.

An opponent jabs or throws straight right.

You time your counter "hook" ensuring your elbow is down.

Their punching arm must miss the target, and the damage is caused by the collision of your forearm at the extended elbow joint, forcing the joint, whist the arm is extended and braced at the opponent's neck.

Result: TKO, broken arm.

Use of Elbow/Forearm:
Years ago, a trainer taught me how to use my forearms and elbows. It is a matter of throwing the hook, inverting your fist so that the top of your hand is facing you as you connect (very like looking for the time on a wrist watch). If you miss, the arc of your forearm means you must connect with part of the elbow or forearm.

I used to practice on the bags in the gym but never ever used it.

I got my nose crushed by a deliberate butt by a fighter coming off the ropes in Bell Green, Coventry. I gave the guy an absolute thrashing without the need to cheat.

Rocky seldom missed with a hook.

Tip: there is a legal use of elbows to block hooks which destroys the opponent's biceps and is extremely effective. The harder an opponent hits, the worse the damage they acquire if their bicep hits the point of your elbow.

Further blocks to the opponent's body attack can utilize a stabbing action down, which often results in hand damage to the opponent.

Timing and practice are required. Fighters like Mayweather incorporate these defensive moves. They really work and can stop the opponent hooking immediately if they are sustaining injury.

Drugs and Hormones:
At one time, I would have said that the use of drugs and hormones was minimal and restricted to heavyweights.

There is the possibility that lighter weights have used H.G.H and other illegal substances to assist in gaining weight and improving recovery and muscle percentage.

How can pre-fight and post-fight tests be written out of professional contracts?

Standing on Feet:
This occurs most often in orthodox southpaw, but is surprisingly effective in restricting the escape of your opponent.

Smelling Salts:
This is forbidden, but most professional cut men/ trainers carry some.

I have a lovely photo of a boxer pointing at the corner administering smelling salts whilst the ref counts over a prone fighter on his back.

Failure to Make Weight:
Some professional fighters deliberately fail to make weight, pay a fine

or compensation to the opponent, and lose the belt on the scales. Fighting with a weight advantage and less stress on their body of making weight, the fight is taken and the lighter fighter may lose badly.

Amateur fighters would lose on the scales and be unable to compete in the tournament.

Both amateur and professional Fighters may have a secondary weigh in to ensure they do not take a huge weight advantage into the ring.

Ringers:
This is not very common but the adoption of the name of another fighter may conceal a fighter's record, age and other facts.

Liniment:
It has been alleged that Liston's corner used liniment on his gloves to blind Ali.

Alcohol:
Liquor has sometimes been smuggled into rings in water bottles to assist a fighter through the final stages of a fight This practice is dangerous, totally illegal, and unlikely to help. In the old days, it was brandy. I would prefer scotch.

I read a story about a fighter in the 1800s who swore by starting his training each day with an egg yolk in sherry and a cracker or dry toast.

How things have changed!

Hostile People at your Corner:
I have experienced hostile "members of the public" actually coming to our corner and had to be very terse.

Extra Corner Members Influencing Judges:
Yelling from a corner to influence judges is kind of a commentary on how well they are doing when their man is missing with punches. We

are setting up a person to yell "he missed" when he misses.

I witnessed a corner deliberately yelling if their fighter did anything. The fighter was throwing punches that clearly missed, yet they screamed approval to the extent the fighter was awarded the contest.

Recently, I saw a fight where a boxer was stunned by a blow. His corner yelled "stop boxing!" and the fighters parted. I have been involved in boxing 50 years and had never seen such a violation.

If I have concerns regarding a fighter or corner I tell the judges and referee prior to the fight.

Taking a Dive:
This was common years ago due to the influence of organized crime, and it is possible even now to pad a record by bribing opponents, I have seen a fighter take a dive for self-preservation caused through fear.

Unbalancing Opponents:
Generations of fighters have learned to nudge with shoulders or brace opponents on the ropes with forearms to render their opponent momentarily off balance.

If they have no balance, they cannot hit, and they are vulnerable.

Equipment You Should Buy

=Quality gloves. Try to buy the best you can afford (16-ounce leather).

-Quality headgear. Make sure it fits well and has a nonslip lining.

-Mouth guard.

-Mexican style 180" wraps.

-Weighted rope. Skip on a smooth surface to protect your rope.

-Chest protector.

-Timer or app.

What to Avoid in a Boxing Club

Clubs doing charity events to make money and obtain members who believe it's all for charity.

Clubs keen on heavy sparring all the time.

Clubs that run classes and charge $100-plus a month.

Instructors with city qualifications and no experience.

Personal trainers at $50 + per hour.

Trainers that drink heavily or take drugs.

Clubs that do not open when advertised.

Pressure to spar.

Sparring at unequal weight, size, or experience.

Weight of glove must be equal (16-ounce) and sparring quality.

Sparring without a trainer present.

Sparring without head guards and mouth guards.

Any club that does not emphasize the importance of balance and movement and fails to concentrate on them before you start to box.

Any club over-rotating ankles for hooks and straight rights. Get the hell out of there!

What to Look for in a Boxing Club

Good coaches who know what they are doing, working in a structured way.

The club must have fighters (not charity events or white collar – real fighters).

Be extremely wary of any club obsessively promoting multiple charity events.

Clubs do not need the latest equipment.

Clubs do not need to be huge.

The club should have a boxing ring.

Punch bags and equipment should be in good shape.

The gym should be clean.

Membership should be reasonably priced with unlimited access.

Avoid class-based memberships. They just want you to get in and out.

Clubs with a great reputation.

Clubs should be chartered members of a boxing association.

Fighters and Features in Force: An Album

ADRIAN BRONER
FOUR WEIGHT WORLD CHAMPION

TOMMY BURNS
CANADIAN-BORN WORLD HEAVYWEIGHT CHAMPION

CARPENTIER VS DEMPSEY
FIRST MILLION DOLLAR PURSE

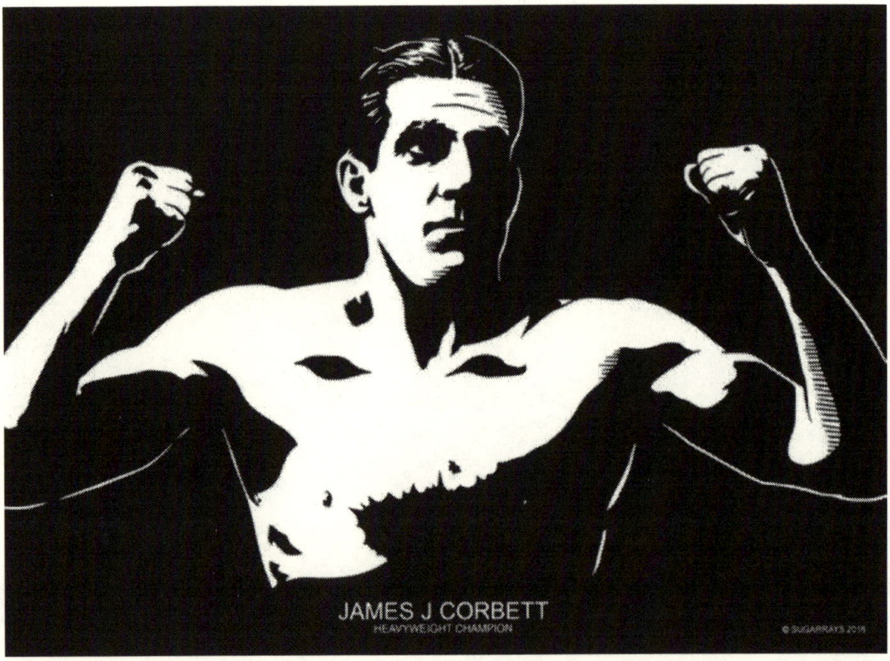
JAMES J CORBETT
HEAVYWEIGHT CHAMPION
© SUGARRAYS 2016

JACK DEMPSEY
WORLD HEAVYWEIGHT CHAMPION 1919-1926

OSCAR DE LA HOYA
FIGHTER OF THE YEAR 1995

BOB FITZSIMMONS
FIRST THREE-DIVISION WORLD CHAMPION

GEORGE FOREMAN
TWO-TIME HEAVYWEIGHT WORLD CHAMPION

SMOKIN JOE FRAZIER
ONE OF THE TEN GREATEST HEAVYWEIGHTS OF ALL TIME

GENADDY GOLOVKIN
RANKED WORLDS NUMBER 1 MIDDLEWEIGHT IN 2016

REG GUTTERIDGE
BOXING JOURNALIST AND TELEVISION COMMENTATOR

MARVIN HAGLER
UNDISPUTED MIDDLEWEIGHT CHAMPION FROM 1980 TO 1987

THOMAS HEARNS
1ST BOXER TO WIN 4 TITLES IN FOUR DIVISIONS

© SUGARRAYS 2016

HOLYFIELD'S BITTEN EAR

VIRGIL HUNTER
TEAM KING BOXING TRAINER

JACK JOHNSON
FIRST AFRICAN AMERICAN WORLD HEAVYWEIGHT BOXING CHAMPION

MILLS BEE LANE III
A RETIRED BOXING REFEREE, AND FORMER BOXER

SAM LANGFORD
CANADIAN BOXER

SUGAR RAY LEONARD
BOXER OF THE DECADE" IN THE 1980'S

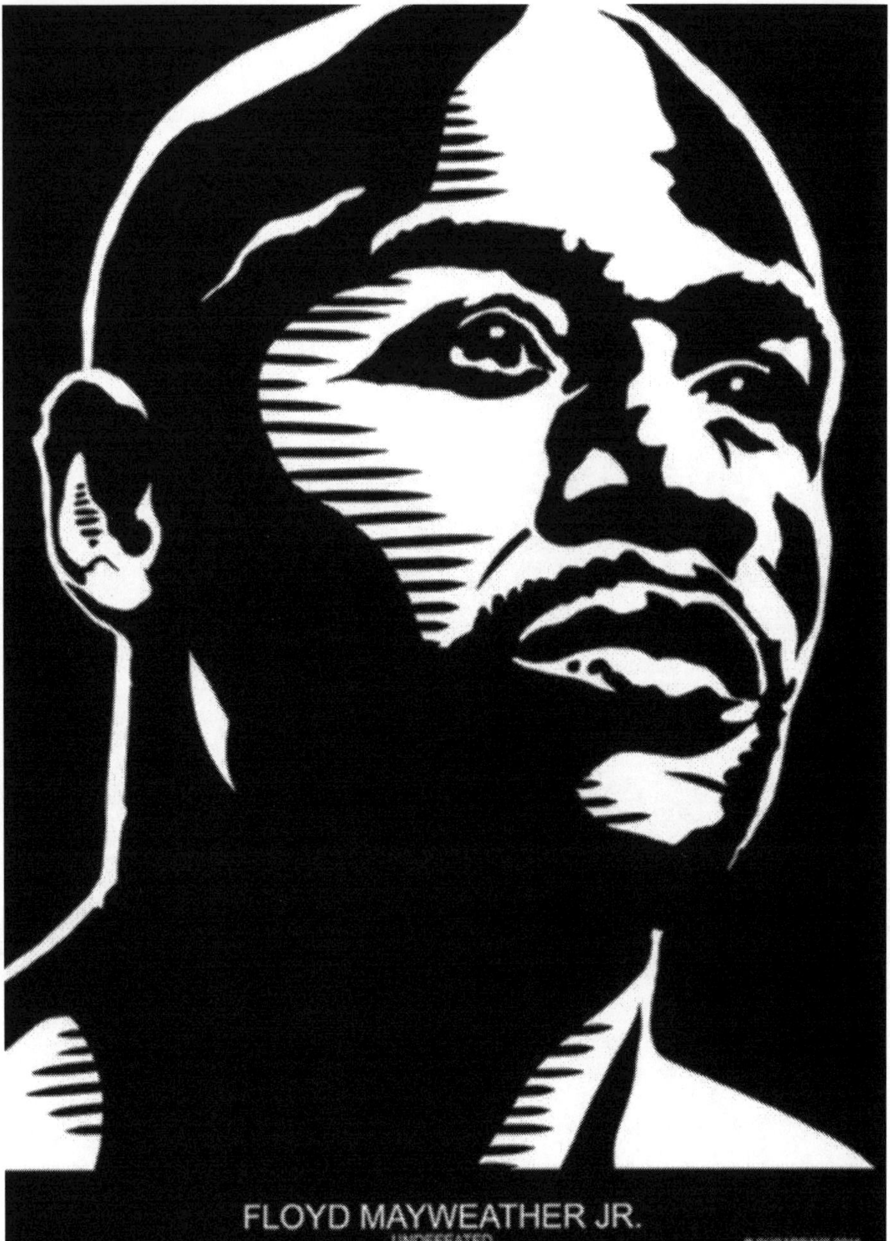
FLOYD MAYWEATHER JR.
UNDEFEATED

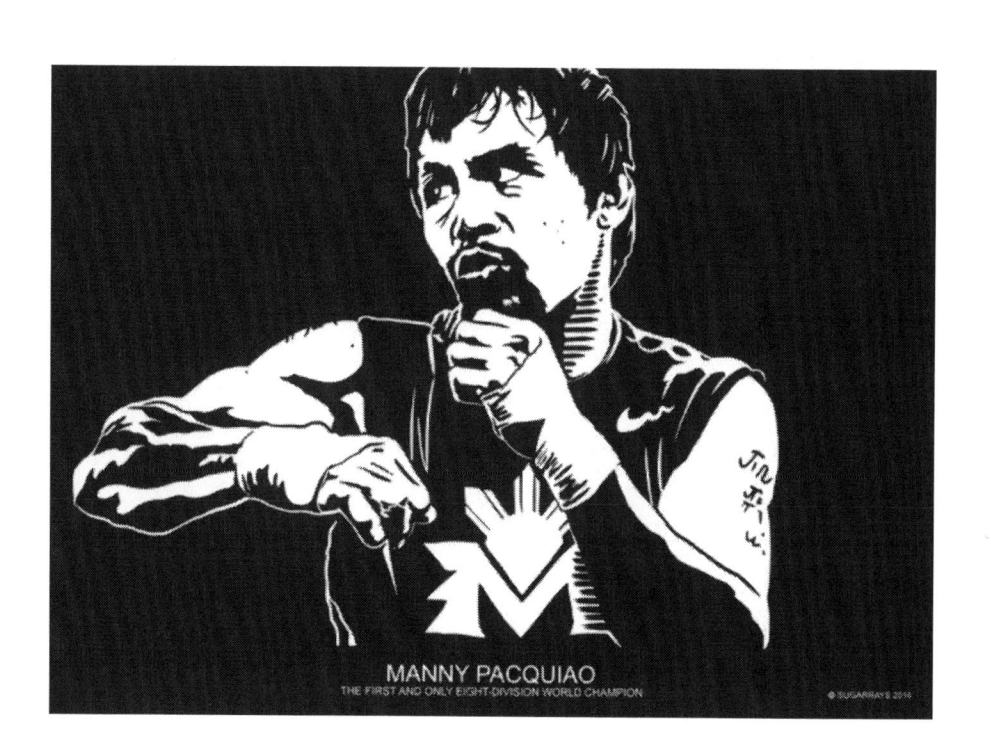

MANNY PACQUIAO
THE FIRST AND ONLY EIGHT-DIVISION WORLD CHAMPION

WILLIE PEP
HELD THE WORLD FEATHERWEIGHT CHAMPIONSHIP TWICE

FREDDIE ROACH
MULTIPLE US TRAINER OF THE YEAR AND POSSIBLY THE GREATEST LIVING TRAINER

BENLEE
SUGAR RAY ROBINSON
FREQUENTLY CITED AS THE GREATEST BOXER OF ALL TIME

EMANUEL STEWARD
AMERICAN BOXER, TRAINER, AND COMMENTATOR

JOHN L SULLIVAN
HEAVYWEIGHT CHAMPION OF AMERICA
© SUGARRAYS 2016

MIKE TYSON
KNOWN AS "THE BADDEST MAN ON THE PLANET"

ANDRE WARD
WON GOLD IN THE 2004 OLYMPICS

Acknowledgements

Thanks to every trainer who spared a little time for me, every fighter for their inspiration, and every student I have worked with. For those special moments, I would do it all again.

I could not finish without paying tribute to the staff and members at Sugarrays Professional Boxing Gym: thanks Sean, Brennan, Zolty, and the boys and girls at Sugarrays.

Finally, thank you to Rich Katynski for his creative artwork and to my editor, Russ Gourluck, who gently steered my work in the right direction.

Bob McAdam

Made in the USA
Middletown, DE
13 April 2018